FORWARD

Human service organizations, like all organizations, are, for the most part, fragile constructions. In essence they are networks of relationships, formal, inform, regular, occasional, to which we have weak or strong ties.

Whatever our relationships are to them, many organizations touch each of our lives on a daily basis, and so their performance matters deeply. That performance is ensured, or not, by its managers.

While the phrase "First, do no harm" is not actually in the original Hippocratic Oath, it is a sentiment that has come into common parlance as a general guide to professional practice wherever. It is my suggestion that all managers take this phrase and place it on their wall. In my teaching research, consultation and participation in issues about management, I see managerial harm inflicted on a daily basis. There is harm to employees, harm to clients and harm to a range of stakeholders. These effects are unacceptable and must be addressed.

In recent years we have seen pensions wiped out as badly run organizations collapsed, deaths in the tens of thousands caused by iatrogenic illnesses, needed aid delivered by tortoise because of managerial incompetence, intraorganizational bickering, and the list goes on. And these are the huge problems; they do not count the hundreds of phone calls each of us make every month to get organizations to minimally do what they were supposed to do in the first place.

I am reminded of a memo I got from an administrator. He sent me a paper and it had the little yellow sticker "SIGN HERE" on the page's bottom. I initialed it and sent it on. Apparently there was an error somewhere in the system. My signature was not only not required, but prohibited. The memo came back attached to another memo which said: "Dr. Tropman, you have erroneously initialed the attached memo. Please erase your initials and initial your erasure."

I do not believe, though, that managers get up in the morning with a plan to ruin peoples lives. For the most part, I believe that they are generally unsure what to actually do. Such uncertainty, when combined with teams of people with the same uncertainty, is a huge source of difficulty. And because of it, many of us reproduce the very patterns we hated when they were inflicted upon us.

I hope this volume can provide some guidance to those managers who wish to avoid the "perp/vic" cycle, perpetrating upon their employees that by which they were once victimized.

John E. Tropman

ACKNOWLEDGEMENTS

It is as true for books as the Academy Awards. Accomplishments are the result of a formal and informal connection, regardless of who is on the cover or the marquee.

I would like to thank my grandchildren Jared, Evelyn, twins Dan and Ethan, and Charlotte. It is a blessing they live near us and we see them many times during the week. It is useful to note, though, that having five kids under six around you, gives a new appreciation for management at the ground level.

I want to thank my daughters Sarah and Jessica, and their husbands Kevin and Matthew. Talking with them about their workplace and homeplace situations also enriches one's perspectives on management, and reinforces the truth that management skills are appropriate whether one is planning an annual meeting or a birthday party with thirteen kids.

My son Matt, who himself is the Executive Director of a nonprofit arts organization was invaluable to me in securing his perspectives.

My wife Penny has been, and is, a continuing source of support and encouragement. She occasionally tells me that my expectations for good treatment at the hands of organizations is unrealistic, and that I am going to (and have) worked myself into a tizzy with unrealistic hopes. She may well be right; my feeling though is that it is appropriate to keep the "best standards" in mind, even if, as we all do, they often fall short.

TABLE OF CONTENTS

INTRODUCTION

Management

Management, wherever it exists, involves accomplishing work through others. In the nonprofit sector, "moving up" is as much a sign of success and approbation as it is in the governmental and corporate worlds. You often start as a worker, or a program assistant, or in some other beginning job where you do that job and are supervised in that job. As time goes on you get more responsibility and "move up". This is when the idea of career comes in, as distinct from the job. A job is a set of tasks that you perform on a regular basis. You can see clients, teach second grade, or sell condos. A career is a succession of jobs, linked over time, which represent advancement and achievement.

You can, of course, have a "flat" career in which you move from one beginning job to another with no sense of advancing or increasing responsibility. You can also have a variegated career, in which you take distinctly different jobs, one after the other, so that the linkage is clear only in retrospect or perhaps, is even non existent. But for most workers, a career represents the line of advancement in which each job fits. In an ideal plan, there is a series of antecedent and subsequent jobs each connecting to and following from one to the other. A career might be at the same agency or organization or it may, and frequently does, involve moving from one organization to a new job at a higher level at another organization.

Career Pathing

Career pathing is the process through which individuals, alone or with a human resources professional, chart their career development over a series of jobs. This process is designed to make job change part of a personal strategic plan rather than a "come what may" approach. Career coaching is the process though which you develop a career path. Job coaching deals with items and concerns with respect to the specific job you have at any one time.

Careers of course do not progress in an upward stream of successes. For one thing, the "smooth" career is rather infrequent in process, though it might look smooth in retrospect. Appropriate next jobs are often not available, something else comes up, or there are personal matters (dual careers, needing a particular school for a particular child, injuries and illness) which cause twists and turns in the career path, making the actual experience warped and jagged.

Moreover, problems of varying kinds occur as you move from job to job. Anxiety can develop when you are under-skilled or under-resourced for a particular job. Boredom emerges when your skills exceed the job you are working on now. Job stagnation develops because of blocks in the system. Even if you remain in the same agency there are boundaries (often not well marked) that you cross in which the previous skills are no longer very useful and new skills are needed. The difficulty of course, is that you get the new job not because you would be good at it but, because you were good at the job you no longer have. Players becoming coaches is a perfect example of this phenomenon. Being a good player in no way means you are a good coach; indeed, the reverse might be the case.

As most employees move out their first job they take on increasing responsibility for the work of others. The first step in this "staircase" might be functional supervision, in which the job of the supervisor is to ensure that new, less experienced or inexperienced workers have someone to guide them in the overall aspects of the job and in the finer points as well. This initial functional supervision is substantive in nature, and while it has aspects of managerial elements (is the proper time being spent with clients; are reports being done correctly?) it is mainly designed to assist the worker in questions that he or she has about doing the job. A problem arises quickly, however, because there is a lot of unevenness in the understanding of this (and other) kinds of supervision. What, exactly, does it mean to assist someone in the carrying out of his or her job? In addition, how much checking and rechecking should you do if you are a supervisor of this type? Moreover, the training and educational programs available for workers as they become managerial supervisors are few, and range from uneven to poor. Most common, perhaps, is a path that simply promotes them into the job, and lets them learn supervision through a combination of on the job training (OJT), and whatever they can cull from their previous experiences. This book will hopefully help you avoid some of the most common pitfalls.

FROM SUPERVISORY MANAGER TO MIDDLE MANAGER:
Tasks and Functions on the Managerial Staircase

Introduction

Management usually begins in one of two ways. Perhaps the most common for those in human services is the role of clinical supervisor. In this role, a worker is promoted to supervisor with the understanding that they will have supervisory responsibility over the content of the work that other workers are doing. Content, in the clinical context, refers to the substance of the workers' activities which includes: how they are interacting with clients; how they are assisting the client on the journey to self-understanding and healing; and the actual ways in which the worker is intervening with the client. This supervision is usually accomplished through case recording, which is either read by the clinical supervisor, done through indirect observation through audio and videotapes, or direct observation through a one way glass. The supervisor and supervisee then analyze material gathered. The clinical supervisor not only "corrects" the supervisee, but also makes suggestions of new approaches, other possible diagnoses, etc.

There are, however, often unclear expectations about whether the clinical supervisor is also a managerial supervisor, responsible for managing the workers' time (e.g. coming on time, meeting agency time guidelines). Naturally, there is no absolutely crisp distinction between them, which only reinforces the importance of the agency doing what few agencies actually do, clarify the concept for the clinical supervisor. Over time, the clinical supervisor usually morphs into a managerial supervisor. Certainly this is true as the supervisor moves up the managerial ladder.

The other way you achieve a supervisory management position is more direct. You are appointed to supervise a specific job as supervisory manager. Whichever of these two paths you take, the appointment to a supervisory management position usually is the first step on a career ladder leading on to project management and then middle management. Let's look at the steps and functions of these three positions. Steps are fairly unique to each position and the functions follow in different proportions.

Three Steps on the Managerial Staircase

1. Supervisory Manager

You are a supervisory manager or managerial supervisor when you are put in charge of one or more persons. Your purpose is to assist them with the accomplishment of their jobs in a timely fashion and according to law and policy.

2. Project Manager

You are a project manager when you are responsible for the completion of a project in the agency which involves sequencing or linking jobs and tasks, and supervise one or more direct reports (or people assigned to work on that project). Project completion within time and budget is the central goal, and the employees' work (or that portion of the employee's work you supervise) is aimed at the accomplishment of that project within temporal, legal and financial constraints. The word task is used here because it suggests that the activities contribute to some larger result.

3. Middle Manager

You are a middle manager when you have more than one project, or a much larger project for which you are responsible. The work of middle management involves attention to the mission of the agency and is made up of bundles of project tasks which are in turn comprised of jobs and assignments. Project managers and middle managers are, like managerial supervisors, additionally charged with encouraging and supporting innovation and invention. The figures below address some of the issues we have discussed in a graphical way (see Figures 1, 2, and 3).

Position, Responsibility, Focus and Activities on the Managerial Staircase

Position	Responsibility	Focus	Activities
1. Supervisory Manager	Jobs	Assignments	Oversight
2. Project Manager	Tasks	Projects	Organize
3. Middle Manager	Work	Systems/Mission	Orchestrate

Figure 1

Devolution of Work into Task and Job Bundles

WORK				
TASK 1	TASK 2	TASK 3	TASK 4	TASK 5
job job job job	job job job job	job job job job	job job job job	job job job job

Figure 2

Devolution of Mission into Project and Assignment Bundles

MISSION				
PROJECT 1	PROJECT 2	PROJECT 3	PROJECT 4	PROJECT 5
assignments	assignments	assignments	assignments	assignments

Figure 3

Functions within the Managerial Staircase

There are five functions involved in the Managerial Staircase.

> 1. adding innovation and invention,
> 2. performing efficiency and effectiveness,
> 3. promoting best practices (identification, harvesting and workout),
> 4. developing in this job and for the next job,
> 5. promoting leadership responsibility for self and agency.
>
> Also see Figure 4 on page 4.

1. Innovation and Invention

Innovation refers to improving the procedures and processes you are already doing. Invention means adding products, treatments, and interventions that you are not doing. Supervisory managers have the responsibility for encouraging innovation among their supervisees. Part of the job of each supervisee is to innovate (to improve the job) and the managerial supervisor needs to oversee that outcome. The managerial supervisor also encourages invention. Project managers also produce innovation as a by-product of their work, and support invention. Middle managers orchestrate these innovations but focus more on developing packages of inventions from the suggestions that the supervisory managers make.

**Differential Focus/Emphasis on Functional Foci
Across the Managerial Staircase**

	Supervisor	Project Manager	Middle Manager
1) adding innovation and invention	Innovation focus 90%	Innovation focus 80%	Invention focus 50% Innovation focus 50%
2) performing efficiently and effectively	Efficiency focus 90%	Efficiency focus 80%	Effectiveness focus 75% Efficiency focus 25%
3) promoting best practices (identification, harvesting and workout)	Best Practice Identification	Best Practice Harvesting	Best Practice Workout Implementation
4) developing in This job and for the Next job	90%This/10% Next	75% This/25% Next	60%This/0% Next
5) promoting leadership: responsibility for self and agency	10% Leadership focus	25% Leadership focus	50% Leadership focus

Figure 4

2. Efficiency and Effectiveness

Efficiency means doing things right. Essentially, it means following the procedures and protocols for job performance. At minimum, efficiency means satisfactory performance. Managerial supervisors work toward producing optimal performance. Effectiveness means doing the right thing. You can be efficient doing incorrect or unnecessary tasks. Hence, the dual focus of the managerial supervisor is to do the right thing, the right way. Project managers and middle managers have a similar focus, except they look at larger venues – the supervisory managers looking at the supervisee, the project managers look at the project and the agency as a whole.

3. Promoting Best Practices (Identification, Harvesting and Workout)

In each workplace, there are people who know how to do particular procedures very well. One problem many organizations have is that they fail to identify these practices in any systematic way. Best practices are harvested at random rather than systematically. Then there is the "people problem" where staff members who are very good at "X" are viewed as odd or unusual. Hence, the message of best practice is not accepted because the person who does it best lacks favor in the agency. Managerial supervisors need to regularly work with each supervisee to determine what they are especially good at and helping them to understand and record their procedures so that others can use them. This practice is called harvesting. It leads to "workout" which means (literally) "taking work out of the system." Managerial supervisors need to help supervisees share their better practices with others.

4. Developing in this Job and for the next Job

Managerial supervisors need to help supervisees develop themselves as professionals in their current job. Supervisees need to become better at what they do, and soon should begin taking on more and different assignments. The managerial supervisor may not or often will not do this by themselves. Rather it means encouraging the supervisee along a path of self-development through trainings, and courses, in particular. What the supervisor does control are the resources that make such undertakings possible and the emotional encouragement and support to actually do it. The supervisor should be prepared with rewards for those who successfully self-develop. Part of the self-development is for the current job, of course, but part of it is really for the next job. Supervisees should always have two jobs in mind – the current one and the next one. Managerial supervisors accomplish this task by working with supervisees to develop a career path which runs out over several years. That way there is a guide to trainings, assignments, etc.

5. Promoting Leadership Responsibility for Self and Agency

Finally, each step on the Managerial Staircase not only supports the step above, but also supports and encourages the level below in taking "leadership" within the organization. However, this is in terms of personal self, and as a part of the overall "leadership" of the agency. Leadership may involve (it usually does involve) some level of risk taking. Of course, what is a risk to one may not be to another, but that is something the managerial supervisor works through with their charges.

A simple example of leadership comes from the best practices harvesting process. When a better practice has been developed and refined, it is ready to be presented to others at the agency, in the local community or in the state or national community. Managerial supervisors encourage supervisees to make such presentations. But leadership is not only a personal thing. Everyone who works for the agency (any agency) has a responsibility to take leadership in helping that agency succeed. As the old phrase has it, "leadership is like manure; it only works when you spread it around!"

Perhaps the most reasonable way to approach the leadership question is to add "agency leadership" (with examples) into the job description of each person who works for the agency. Many employees feel that their job is basically their only function within the organization. For one example, I can offer the CFO of an agency who felt that her job was, simply, to be the CFO. She was fired because she could not become a member of the top team in any sense larger than that of the financial person. When she was asked about the agency as a whole, her response was "That is for others (I am not sure which "others") to decide." She was unable, and unhelped, to step up to the larger role of agency leader in her role as CFO. Each of us, at any level large or small, has a leadership role.

Conclusion

The managerial supervisor is the first step on the Managerial Staircase leading from project manager to middle manager. The core of the supervisory responsibility is the job of the supervisee, on the assignments they have, and on overseeing that the assignments are completed and fit into the job package appropriately. This bundle becomes more general at the project manger level and the middle manager level (see Figure 1 on page 2).

While these foci tend to be unique at each level, some functions exist across all levels, such as the following:

1. adding innovation and invention,
2. performing efficiency and effectiveness,
3. promoting best practices (identification, harvesting and workout),
4. developing in this job and for the next job, and
5. promoting leadership responsibility for self and agency.

Part 1 - Chapter 1

SUPERVISION, PROJECT MANAGEMENT, AND MIDDLE MANAGEMENT: Some Crucial Techniques

Introduction

Supervisory management oversees activities of the job, whether as a part of a clinical supervisor's job or as a solo job function, . The supervisor manages outputs (activities and events) to outcomes (results). The organization of a supervisor's work in terms of the agency itself may vary. A supervisor may oversee all of an employee's (or multiple employees') work. Alternatively, a supervisor may also supervise other professionals in a unit with a particular function. In addition, a supervisor may be assigned a portion of the 24 hour day for which they are responsible.

The project manager has a particular product or event for which they are responsible. This particular product or event has a budget of money, people, supplies, and expectations toward which project managers work. There is usually a team of employees assigned to the project, though it may not be a dedicated team. A dedicated team is one which 100% of the team members' time is assigned to the project. A project could be an ongoing agency function, like intake or the annual meeting, or it could be a one time event such as installing a new computer system or a special community appreciation event. Some members of the project team may supervise other members of the team. A manager is one who has several projects under his or her direction which, together make up a significant part or element of the agency's product line. An agency therefore might have a manager of adoptions, a manager of foster care, a manager of food service, a manager of facilities, etc.

Changes and Dangers As You Go

As you move through and up the ranks of management, the tools of the previous stage are retained, and new tools are added to the mix. It is vital that an appreciation of the previous set of tools be retained, even if the application is less than before. One mistake that employees make is to think that their next job is like their former job, only bigger. This misperception leads, perversely, to the increased application of the previous signature elements rather than the decreased use of them. For example, one of the essential (perhaps the most essential) element in supervision is oversight, "inspect what you expect" is the popular phrase. However, as you move to project management, dates and deliverables become a core focus and supervision is handled much more by others or by the employee.

Span of control (how many people you can actually oversee [commonly thought to be five]) often migrates to span of communication (employees that come to you when they need you). But if the new project manager misperceives the mission, and thinks that more oversight is needed, they often lose focus on the overall project and that irritates the employees. Similarly, motivational enhancement (getting work done through others) is the essence of the manager's job. Too much checking (micromanaging) or over focus on dates and deliverables means that the middle manager is not doing the motivational task.

The Necessity of Management

Management makes the world go round, though often poorly. Whatever level of management you are currently at (supervisory, project, or middle), you should start with the understanding that your work is vital to the persons, agencies, and communities whom you serve and the nations, society, and world in which you reside. Why is it so important? Is telling people what to do that crucial? If you answer these questions using the initial understanding of management just mentioned, then the answer is no. But a more profound definition of management, harmonizing systems for efficient and effective outcomes – changes the answer to yes. The insight is that the manager's focus is systems not persons. This statement is true even as you work daily with many individual persons. Another insight is that the persons with whom you work are, mainly, messengers of the systems in which they are functioning, or enmeshed. Edwards Deming made the point this way: of all the results we see, 85% of them are due to "common causes of variation" in the system, and 15% are due to individual causes of variation in the person (Deming, 1982).

The excellent manager stresses the common causes and attends to the individual causes. Managerial supervisors are working with the person; project managers with several persons and other elements; the middle manager with several projects. These are all systems (Tropman and Schuester, 2000). Working to harmonize systems is vital to good work and successful living whether it is value systems in conflict, antique behavioral systems not attuned to best practices, tensions among and between project staff, conflicts over resources among projects, or others. This is the manager's important work, harmonizing systems!

Managerial META Mission

General system responsibility leads to some general duties. According to Sayles and Chandler, in their book Managing Large Systems (1971; 1992) the manager has a generalized set of responsibilities that encompass all other more specific ones. To my thinking, these apply, albeit at different levels and in different amounts, to all managerial and executive work. The manager's set of responsibilities include:

> 1. taking problems at the right time
> 2. taking problems in the right order
> 3. setting and changing decision criteria
> 4. acting as an organizational metronome

1. Taking Problems at the Right Time:

This phrase means knowing at what point a problem needs to be addressed. Timing can be a result of many elements. One is project flow, which is specifically discussed in the next point. Another reason relates to interpersonal and emotional readiness. For example, in the case of bad news, staffs tend to go through a reaction often referred to as SARAH. SARAH stands for Shock, Anger, Rejection, Acceptance, and Help. Managers trying to help too early, during the shock, anger and rejection (denial) phases can be very nonproductive. It is better to wait until some measure of acceptance has been achieved; then help is usually welcomed. In addition, there is the question of resources. Sometimes, if you have a bit of extra resource, it "creates" the right time.

2. Taking Problems in the Right Order:

This refers to a "hierarchy of needs" over time. We need to address certain problems before others can be addressed. Managers need to be sure that antecedent procedures and processes are ready so that subsequent ones can begin. Two concepts relevant here are the Guttmann Scale and the Critical Path.

The Guttmann Scale is an array of tasks, A through I, which has the property that A impacts B through I, B impacts C through I, but not A or B, and so on. This dominance hierarchy of tasks needs to be observed because, if not, there will need to be a lot of rework in the system. If you complete C, and then D through I, THEN do A, and discover that A impacts C, then the C through I subset has to be redone.

The Critical Path is a period between two tasks such as, the amount of time you have to do it is exactly the amount of time you need to do it. For example, if a worker is driving to a court hearing and it typically takes one hour to get there, and the worker leaves only one hour before the hearing, then all will be well if nothing goes wrong. The alert manager will coach workers to leave a bit of extra time just so that if Murphy's Law decides to spring into action there will be some wiggle room.

3. Setting and Changing Decision Criteria:

This reflects the basis on which workers make decisions. In child welfare, for example, child safety is one criterion, but keeping families together is another criterion. While these may not always clash, there will be times when they are at odds, and managers need to clarify the weight of each. Apart from the particularistic instances of conflict, managers need to give general priorities. Moreover, there are many of these kinds of instances for example resource constraints, time constraints, and quality constraints. These each conflict with the other and managers need to articulate appropriate priorities and then, when appropriate, change them.

4. Acting as an Organizational Metronome:

This involves setting the level of urgency by which things are done and the pace at which the organization works. Some organizations operate at a pokey pace. Things are promised in time frames that seem much longer than are needed. The whole organization seems to operate as if in slow motion, or under water. The agency is not lean and mean; it is thick and chatty. Even the employees seem to walk slowly. "Whenever" is the operative phrase. Other organizations seem crisp and prompt; things happen lickety-split. Managers set and exemplify this pace and set the organization's metronome.

POSSBE: The Managerial Tool Kit

All supervision and management involves a tool kit commonly called POSSBE – Planning, Organizing, Strategizing, Staffing, Budgeting and Evaluating. These are the essential tools of the supervisory trade, and ones that are used throughout the managerial career albeit at increasing levels of generality. You do not always proceed through them in this order, although it is the usual order. A job is laid out in broad strokes, with the goals and the steps in rough sequence. The plan morphs into organization, which involves more specificity about the kinds of activities needed to make the plan come to fruition. Strategizing looks at the key elements of the plan, and makes a series of decisions about sequence and fit. Staffing contemplates the people the project needs while budgeting contemplates the dollars needed. Evaluation involves constant review and readjustment based on change circumstances. It is important to note here that budgeting is a ways along in the process. This location is no accident. Money is always the servant of goals, not the reverse. Early discussion of finances is usually too big a burden for projects, as realistic figures cannot be ascertained until you are into the project a bit. Of course, it is also the case that there is feed forward and feed backward process going on in POSSBE dynamic; each phase is influenced by information from "downstream" as well as new inflows from "upstream."

Planning

Planning involves setting the goals. As Steven Covey says, "Start with the end in mind" and the general steps to get there, in an overall way (Covey, 1990). All planning has this component, from planning your day, to planning a course of treatment, to planning your evening meal, to planning an annual meeting, to planning whatever. It is vital to understand that without planning, which involves initial goal setting, nothing else works very well (POSSBE). The other phases require the discipline of a plan. However, it should also be reemphasized that the plan is really a guideline, not a cement overcoat. Criticisms of planning usually overstate the firmness of the plan and then from this "straw person" perspective, point out that it was/is foolish to plan because the context is so ever-changing and dynamic. It is of course true that you want to avoid bad planning, such as over rigidity. Good managerial supervisors invite their supervisees to present their plan for goal achievement (in draft form) and then begin a discussion with them based on that plan. Exceptions to this guideline come when the law or the agency sets requirements (for example, number of sessions). In this case the planning is already done. Planning addresses, but does not always "answer," these questions:

> * What are we going for here?
> * What are our goals or desired outcomes?
> * What is the general procedure by which these ends might be achieved?

Organizing

Organizing adds flesh to the skeleton of planning. After agreement on an initial plan, the supervisor decides which organizational structure can make the plan happen. Organization refers not only to agency organization and patterns of action, but personal ones as well. Managers sometimes call organizing "Operational Planning."

Strategizing

In all human affairs, some things matter more than others. Managers need to help workers "know when to hold 'em" and "know when to fold 'em." Situations have risks and rewards and both need to be considered. Problems can become opportunities – but you need to think about how that could develop. As supervisees enters a particular situation they need to have an exit strategy if the worst happens. In addition, they need to have a capitalization strategy if the best happens. Options need to be available ahead of time, like clothes in your wardrobe. According to "When It Hits the Fan" (Myers, 1981), the person with some plans in his or her pocket is usually better off. But strategies and strategic plans should be guidelines rather than straightjackets. The essence of strategy is focused flexibility. Strategizing discussions with supervisees contemplates questions like these:

- Who is doing what and when?
- What might get in the way?
- What resources do you need?
- How will you monitor your progress?
- What early warning signs or issues should you keep an eye out for?

Staffing

Staffing involves consideration of the people needed to accomplish a task. Staffing answers the question of "who?" Who will we need for this project, and when? What kind of team needs to be assembled? What is the skill mix we will need? Sometimes a project involves many people – some permanent and some moving in and out as needed. Other times it seems there is "just" or "only" a single person on the team. But "seems" is the critical word here. Even in situations where there is apparently one person, there are already two – the supervisee and the supervisor and then others to whom each has access on a limited basis, including informal personal contacts.

Budgeting

Budgeting involves the allocating of resources over the life of jobs, projects, and work. The main resources we allocate are money and time. Typically, time involves "hidden inventory" or the time of people, yours included. Budgeting is typically in several senses a control function. When you budget, you look to the future, both in terms of the input of temporal and financial resource, and their output. A budget is a transition matrix, if you will, morphing anticipated inputs into anticipated outputs (allocations). Of course, there are uncertainties throughout these processes. For example, money does not come in or exceeds expectations. Expenses are different from those anticipated; time becomes gobbled up by this, that, and the other thing. But the need to prestructure these allocations (even in a general way) is crucial to management at all levels. Budgets not only provide controls, they also provide goals or targets toward which investments should be made. For example, an organization's goal may be to hold its annual meeting for $10,000. This goal can be a control as the organization only has $10K available for this event.

Financial matters are not the only ones that need budgeting; time needs budgeting as well. Time management is nothing more (or less) than a time budget. Like a money budget, it controls the amount of time spent on an item, and may also be a goal to meet or exceed (in this case "exceed" means "be lower than") the budgeted amount. Time budgets become crucial in work where there are not natural temporal boundaries. For example, a class is scheduled to be a certain number of hours long. When I teach a class, I have to fit my material into the available time, as others will be using the room after me and students have other commitments. But much of human service work and non-profit work does not have such boundaries. The following two examples illustrate this point.

1. In dealing with client needs, there is usually no limit to what you could offer. Hence you, as a worker, need to set the limits of the possible. Managerial supervisors also need to assist workers in doing that. Correlatively, managerial supervisors need to assist supervisees in not feeling bad about not doing more, but instead, feeling good about what they were able to do.

2. A second example, and one we shall discuss in more detail later, is meetings. Time and meetings are a real problem, both in terms of the time spent on any item within a meeting, and the total number of hours spent in these meetings. Managerial supervisors, project managers, and middle managers need to run excellent meetings, whether they are a one on one meeting, a staff meeting, or any meeting. A time budget is a great place to start. The experience of the supervisor can help the supervisee estimate how much time different tasks will take (and the supervisor can suggest how much they should take), and develop the steps that will help the supervisee to accomplish the tasks in the time available. Making and recording these decisions, and then reviewing the allocations of money and time to ascertain if they are in the budgeted ballpark is the essence of budgeting.

Evaluating: Feedback and Grading

The last function in the POSSBE acronym is evaluating. Socrates' dictum that "the unexamined life is not worth living" applies in modified form to supervision as well. Managerial supervision is a constant process of goal setting, monitoring, overseeing, assessing, and appraising. No evaluation process is possible without goals established at the front end. Typically, these goals are mutually agreed upon between the supervisee and the managerial supervisor. Following that, monitoring which can be formal or informal, involves benchmarks that need to be accomplished by the supervisee and/or the supervisor so the process can move forward. These can be relatively automatic. Oversight (inspect what you expect) consists of periodic check-in meetings during which the supervisor and the supervisee can assess the extent to which everyone is on target. If oversight is quarterly, then assessment is a mid course meeting during which the overall progress is judged. There is a third quarter oversight meeting, and then a final "performance appraisal" during which goal achievement is checked and a "grade" given.

Evaluation has two dimensions which run through this process – feedback and grading. Feedback consists of simple tips on how the supervisee's performance might be improved. Grading reflects a qualitative, though evidence-based, judgment on how well the supervisee did. The front end of the evaluation process is heavily feedback centered; as time moves along, evaluation becomes more important, and in the appraisal meeting evaluation is the most powerful component. Grading involves judgment, working to standard (or above standard), is a situation where the grader is more powerful than the gradee. Of all tasks, managers seem to hate performance appraisal the most, and do it poorly and infrequently, if at all. This task avoidance sets off a negative self fulfilling prophecy in which there is little experience, which results in task avoidance, which in turn results in limited experience, which in its turn results in more avoidance, etc. It is no wonder performance appraisal is heartily disliked by everyone in organizations. Yet there are people who are good at performance appraisal. Music teachers, cooking instructors, and coaches are but a few examples of professions where evaluation is a constant, ongoing process. It can be done well, and for high quality work must be done well. We will discuss more about "feedback communication" in chapter 14.

Managers also need assessment themselves. One good approach is a 360° approach. In this method, the manager secures feedback from subordinates, superiors, peers, the external network, and his or her own self (and family). The results are usually given to an outside person who digests them and presents feedback on patterns to the manager.

Tips for the Manager

There are lots of ways in which managers can improve the work they do, whether it is supervisory management, project management, or middle management. Many of these will be shared through the volume, but six of the most general ones are as follows:

1) Managing By Wandering Around (MBWA)

Developed by Tom Peters, this concept encourages managers to get out of their office and touch base with workers and others informally (Peters & Waterman, 1982). It is useful for monitoring and oversight. MBWA is helpful because it gets you out of your office, and away from the trappings of power that your office conveys. There are some important elements to remember when practicing MBWA. One is to not "react" to what you see and hear at that time. Store it away and if it is necessary, talk with the worker later in private. Remember, that in today's cubicle culture, worker cubicles are not a good place to do serious business.

2) The Eight Ball Principle

This principle addresses the question of ways in which you might achieve goals while at the same time increasing the probability of achieving other goals. These considerations address both "here and now" issues as well as "there and then" issues. You might choose to do something NOW because the potential to help you LATER is enhanced; this is called the "eight ball principle." Pool players will recognize it immediately. A good shot is sinking your target. A better shot is sinking your target and positioning your cue ball for the next shot. The best shot is selecting your target on the basis of positioning, which not only includes the immediate next shot but the next several shots may block your opponent as well.

3) Walk the Talk/Integrity

Walking the talk means, simply, that you do what you say you are going to do. That is a definition of integrity in anyone's book. Example is, perhaps, the most powerful teacher. It is essential that you follow through on your commitments if you want others to do the same. Furthermore, it is simply the right thing to do.

4) The Pinball Principal

Tracy Kidder developed this principle in his book: "The Soul of a New Machine" (1981). He uses it to explain why engineers worked day and night to build a new computer with little additional financial reward. They did it because their success entitled them to more notice and more projects of interest. His general formulation, applicable to all managers, is that praise and support for employees goes a long way. Use it!

5) Two Ears/One Mouth

We have two ears and one mouth; whatever else, that ratio is a useful guide to listening/ talking behavior. Generally, managers should listen twice as much as they talk. Talking is one of those cases where, often, "less is more."

6) Uncertainty Absorption/Authoritative Augmentation

As managerial supervisors, project managers, and middle managers, you have more power than those below you. This power differential creates two truths. The first is uncertainty absorption. As March and Simon discuss it (1959) uncertainty absorption refers to the inference structure of an organization. "Uncertainty absorption occurs when inferences are drawn from a body of evidence and then the inferences, instead of the evidence itself, are then communicated" (March and Simon, 1958: p.165). Moreover, I would add, communicated as fact, with particular emphasis on removing or narrowing the variance. I feel a more useful application for managers comes from examining the accuracy of information reported from subordinates.

When communicating up, subordinates apparently have a preferred sequence of information they like to present: good news, bad news, and then uncertain news. The last is least desirable because of the fact that the messenger feels he or she looks worst in that case. Hence, as subordinates "report up" they have a tendency to convert the uncertain areas into more certain ones, and probabilities (with lots of variance) become certainties (either good or bad). So recall, managers, that the information you get is almost always more "firm" than is actually the case. Authoritative augmentation also involves adding certainty; it just flows the other way. Tentativeness on the part of supervisors and managers (I wonder if …?, Could it be that…?, Would you look into….?, etc) morphs into certainty (Jim insists that…!; Lloyd says do it…! etc.). Tentativeness at the top becomes imperatively certain at the bottom.

Conclusion

Management is the art of getting work done through others. Middle management orchestrates the projects of project managers. Project managers organize resources to accomplish tasks. Project managers depend upon managerial supervisors to oversee the jobs which make up the projects.

Part 2

ORGANIZATIONS: The Setting of Administrative Work

Introduction

Managerial work occurs in formal organizations. However, that is not the only place you manage. Management occurs, of course, with yourself (a topic on which I shall have more to say in Chapter 4), in the family (managing relationships, managing family finances, etc), in neighborhood and community events, and so on. My focus here is on the formal organizational elements of management. However, as readers may have already figured out, management techniques have a lot of generality. What is useful in the organization is useful in the family and the community, and, of course, the reverse. You have to be careful though; treating your spouse or partner as a "worker" is likely to lead to trouble; treating employees as "family" is similarly problematic. Crossovers need to be customized. And of course, managing yourself is always important.

Organizational structure is important because it, rather than individuals, as such, produces the results (or does not produce the results) we hope to achieve. As mentioned before, the famous quality guru Edwards Deming argues that 85% of what the organization produces is organization-driven, and only 15% can be attributed to individuals. Deming calls these "common causes of variation" and "unique causes of variation" (Deming, 1982). The reason it is so important for us to talk about the organization lies in this insight. Further, American society tends to think about the way things work in exactly the opposite way. We prioritize and privilege the individual rather than attending to the organizational (and social) structure. That means we are focusing on "Harry" when we should be looking at "Harry's department."

For management, within formal organizations, it is therefore important to understand more than a little about the structure of formal organizations. Management may, indeed, be "getting work done through others," but it is the connections among the others, and the sequences of those connections, that make a huge difference. A bunch of wonderful people do not, per se, make a wonderful agency. We need to understand some of the unique elements of nonprofit organizations (the next chapter addresses this issue).

A Taste of Organizational Theory

Organizations are one of the forms through which society organizes itself; formal organizations have some common features. As we look at the disciplines of social science, each has its contribution to make in understanding organizations and, its view of them.

Anthropology

Anthropology looks at the culture of organizations, their ideas, values, norms, and beliefs. It tends to see organizations as "patterns of culture." This phrase was the title of a famous anthropological work by Ruth Benedict (1934). Feelings and commitments are important.

Economics

This discipline tends to look at organizations as if they were composed of rational individuals maximizing their own fortunes. Winner take all is key.

Political Science

The political scientist sees the organization as a field of power. Organizational members see power as their currency and seek to maximize power.

Psychology

Psychologists tend to view the organization from the drama of men's and women's "insides." What is their temperament, their "emotion quotient," their communication style? Organizations are viewed as packages of individual characteristics.

Sociology

Sociologists, somewhat like anthropologists, see systems and interconnections of systems and subsystems as key. Their view is that the product of the organization is delivered by the system itself and individual employees are the messengers.

Obviously, these are so brief as to be close to unhelpful. On the other hand, disciplines DO have different prisms through which they look at the world, and it is important to keep that in mind as we proceed.

The Organization

Various thinkers have tried to define or describe organizations. Max Weber (1946) is perhaps the most famous. He talked of organizations having the following elements:

- Division of Labor
- Administrative Apparatus
- Hierarchy of Authority
- Impersonal Rules
- Full Time Jobs/Careers

Most of us can relate to these elements, but in fact they describe the more professional, mature, or developed organizational forms. Organizations at the beginning of the organizational growth cycle (entrepreneurial organizations) may have minimal division of labor, elementary administrative apparatus, murky authority structure, personal rules, and unclear jobs with uncertain career potential. Indeed, one of the challenges for organizations is to form this unorganized beginning into a more formal structure. A challenge for managerial supervisors is to adapt their working style to the entrepreneurial as well as the professional organization.

Another organizational analyst, Robert Quinn (1988) looked at organizations in terms of core elements – the clan, the bureaucracy, the market, and the adhocracy. The clan organization was defined by loyalty and commitment, like a fraternity. The bureaucracy was defined by rules, and doing the same thing thousands of times. It is most like the model mentioned a moment ago by Weber. The market organization, opposite of the clan, is defined only by results; "What have you done for me today?" is the hallmark question. The adhocracy (from the Latin ad hoc, or to this) are organizations driven by ideas and doing the new, single thing. A challenge for managerial supervisors is to articulate supervision goals both to the dominant culture of the organizational type mentioned here, but at the same time effect a balance. After all, in the final analysis organizations cannot be just one thing.

Bohlman and Deal (2003) talk of perspectives or views as ways to understand organizations. The word they use is "frame." They have three frames they consider important: the human resource (people) frame; the political (power, conflict) frame, and the symbolic (cultural) frame. Each "prism" yields a different truth about the organization. Managerial supervisors need to consider each perspective in going about their work – people, power, and culture.

In my own work, I have developed a template, which is useful in looking at organizations (Tropman, 2002). I call it the five "C" template.

1. Characteristics - Who are the people of the organization and what are they like?
2. Competencies - What are the competencies (knowledge + skill) needed for and possessed in the organization?
3. Conditions - What is the structure and culture of the organization?
4. Context - What are the external forces (markets, etc) impinging on the organization?
5. Change - What are the change forces and resistance forces with which the organization must cope?

The challenge for managerial supervisors is to keep these levels and forces in mind as you work with supervisees.

Organizations have formal and informal elements. The formal elements are what we call the Organizational Chart. It reflects one aspect of the organization, one truth, as it were. While it may not mean everything, it means a lot. On the other hand, organizations have informal elements. The informal elements reflect those connections that cross formal organizational lines and through which communication flows. They also reflect who likes whom, who is the "go to" person on what subjects, who will work the extra mile, etc. The "go-to" person is a person with special expertise to which some people in the agency "go to" when they have need of that special expertise. The informal system is the repository of lots of personal information about people in the organization, and also the place where judgments about the quality and character of each person are made and kept. It is also the locus of gossip. Managers and supervisors need to be aware of both elements and the appropriate use of either, depending on the situation.

Finally, organizations have both task and process foci. A "task focus" is one which stresses organizational goals (outputs and outcomes), accomplishments, and achievements. A "process focus" is one which stresses the emotional and social climate of the organization, and attends to items like "compassion at work." Often employees in the agency specialize in contributing in one or the other foci. Frequently, the process contributor (the one who organizes birthday parties for staff, who announces deaths of staff members, who provides office decorations, who sets a food contribution system for employees who are ill, etc.) is very much underappreciated for those leadership roles. Both foci are needed; the "process" foci are often what makes an agency "a great place to work." Managers need to celebrate and reward those who contribute in that way as well as those who sustain organizational goals.

Any or all of these approaches (and others) can be helpful. The important thing for managerial supervisors to recognize is that organizations, as entities, have a reality of their own and managerial supervisors need to work within that reality (or not) to achieve their goals. Supervision does not just "hang" there. Managerial supervisors enact supervision within an organizational context and with certain forces acting upon it.

The Dark Side of Organizations

We all know that organizations have their "dark side." Organizations can develop lots of problems in their functioning, some of which become part of their very character. While I cannot mention all of them here, there are some that are worth special mention.

Oligarchy is one. Organizations small and large tend to be "run" by a small group. This tendency generates a tension between openness and involvement of employees, on the one hand, and "my way or the highway" on the other. Authority, which is generally a good thing, can easily become authoritarian, which is not a good thing.

Organizations develop means (outputs) to achieve ends (outcomes). It is fairly common for some displacement to occur, in which either means replace ends, means continue when ends have changed, or any means are used to justify ends.

Organizations require policy and practice systems to accomplish their tasks. When the distance between these two systems becomes too great, the organization becomes sort of schizoid, and employees get two sets of directives – one the formal way, and the other, the informal way. This is a situation in which the organization itself becomes "crazy making" and where no one is sure what is said is the truth. De Vries and Miller call this type of firm or agency the "neurotic organization" (1984; 1990). It is characterized by unhealthy and troubling organizational patterning.

The "pathology" of organizations is not only something that drives employees crazy; it also causes a lot of harmful behavior to the social system in which it lives. The film, "The Corporation" deals with such abuse. It is based on the book, "The Corporation: The Pathological Pursuit of Profit and Power" by Joel Baken. A.O. Scott, writing a review of the film in the New York Times (2004) says,

> The film…half-mockingly offers a psychiatric diagnosis based on a list of abuses that arise from the relentless pursuit of profit. The point is not that individual companies pollute the environment, hurt animals, exploit workers, and commit accounting fraud, but that such outrages are a result of the essential personality traits of the corporate life form. These behaviors are symptoms arising from a list of pathologies that includes "disregard for the well being of others," "inability to form lasting relationships," and "deceitfulness." A psychiatrist who has advised the F.B.I. declares the corporation has "all the characteristics of a prototypical psychopath" (2004: p/B5).

All natural and social systems require good information if they are to survive and flourish. Predators need to know where prey live and how to catch them; prey needs to know the patterns of predators and how to avoid them. The survival of each depends upon good (but not complete) information. Organizations and agencies as well need information, and they need to discuss and act on that information. In particular the organization needs to address "bad news" in whatever form it takes – financial, human resources, customer/consumer dissatisfaction, etc. Organizations, like the individuals who comprise them often tend to deny bad news and not discuss it, because they fear the consequences that might emerge from that discussion.

Chris Arygris points out, in his book "Strategy, Change and Defensive Routines" (1985), that the oligarchy which controls organizations and agencies often engages in practices where the managerial supervisors fail to discuss key items and engage in "defensive routines." Essentially, defensive routines mean that some things in organizations (and by extension, families) are not discussed. Additionally, their non-discussability is not discussed. One organizational wag calls this kind of behavior "re-arranging deck chairs on the Titanic." Usually the organization or family flounders along until some public disaster strikes (the executive fled with his secretary and the endowment!).

Defensive routines "support" a failure to act on information. They are close to the Boiled Frog Effect (discussed in further Chapter 12), which alleges that if you place a frog in a pan of cold water and slowly raise the temperature of that water over a Bunsen burner, the frog will not notice that it is getting hotter, and will remain and boil to death. Alternatively, if you place a frog in a pan of hot water it will jump right out. In organizational analysis, this frog problem is called the "just noticeable difference syndrome." Some agencies never act on information that is not really different from the last time they looked at it. Hence, significant trends are missed. Environments around organizations are always changing. If they change quickly the organization will usually try to respond. If they are changing slowly, it may be more dangerous because today never looks that different from yesterday. Again, managers delay action until something hits the fan. Managers need to know that avoidance of problems is generally not a good strategy.

Psychic Income and Impaired Dignity at Work

Organizations are made up of people (and other resources). As employees, we spend a lot of time working in organizations. It is about 1/3 of our week, not counting 56 hours for sleep. That of course is based upon a 40 hour week and many work more hours than that. Hence, what happens at work is of great importance to us as people. Of central concern is our meaning and dignity. I have called the meaning element "psychic income," and it turns out to be very important to employees (Tropman, 2001). Employees like to have a meaningful job. That is one part of "psychic income." The other part is to be treated well at work and by work. Randy Hodson (2001) calls this latter "dignity at work." His research identifies ways in which dignity is impaired and workplaces soured. Readers will relate, I am sure, to situations in which dignity has been impaired or destroyed. Here is a thumbnail of Hodson's organizational situations in which workers are left "undignified."

1. The abusive manager, who is either interpersonally (physically or emotionally) abusive or who is abusive through the lack of provision for a coherent workplace.
2. Overwork: also known as, exploiting workers and getting them to work cheap or for free. Overwork occurs where agencies extract work from employees while denying them choice or compensation. The first is called conscription, the second, exploitation. Some kinds of overwork are compensated such as "forced overtime." Workers are conscripted to work extra time, odd times, night shifts, etc. That is not exactly exploitation – except that choice is lost. There are other kinds of overwork that are exploitative however, if you accept my definition of exploitation as

(continued)

"getting employees to work cheap or for free." This kind of overwork is actually quite prevalent in the human service system. Sometimes this is called "commitment" ("Sally will always go the extra mile"). Of course it is good to go the extra mile – occasionally. But there are agencies (and managerial supervisors must guard against becoming a part of this) where going the extra mile is considered appropriate behavior. When that happens agencies are exploiting workers, and extracting labor without compensation.

3. Autonomy constraint or a lack of autonomy. Micromanagement, over checking, etc. are problematic in themselves, and tend to actually produce the errors they are claiming to prevent, and convey to the worker that they are not trustworthy. The noninvolvement or problematic involvement of employees is the difficulty.[1] All workers, but especially professional workers, do have and need to lay some part in how they do their job. Once goals are given, workers enjoy a feeling of means freedom – a sense that they can approach doing the job within the ways of their own choosing (within appropriate agency and legal limits, of course). When that autonomy is constrained through micro managing, for example, workers feel and are, devalued, and undignified.

American society was, and is, the country of "No Taxation Without Representation." That political truism is true, as well, in the organization. Employees like and need to be involved. After all, the closer you are to a problem the more information about it you can provide. Managers who avoid involving employees are not only failing to take available information into account, they are asking for trouble. But perhaps worse is fake or inauthentic involvement. Fake involvement occurs when management has already made up their mind, but asks employees anyway.

4. Rascally Coworkers is where dignity is impaired or destroyed. We like to "get along" with those who work with us – that does not mean we have to be close friends (though work is perhaps THE source of friendships). Coworkers can be bosses, peers, or subordinates. Coworkers who exhibit hostility, seem pushy or deceitful, who are rude and egotistical, etc. make life hell at work.

Difficult coworkers can cause especially great workplace stress. Muriel Solomon (1990) has one of the best volumes on dealing with difficult people. She identifies the following ten categories[2] in Figure 5 on page 24. In discussing each category she addresses the boss, subordinate or peer expression of these problematic behavioral styles. Bramson (1981,1992) deals with similar material in "Coping With Difficult People and Coping with Difficult Bosses."

Solomon's 10 Categories of Difficult People and How to Deal With Them

1) Hostile / angry / belligerent	Ask "Is there anything else?" Try not to let their anger create anger in you.
2) Pushy / presumptuous / arrogant	Set narrow limits; remind them that others have needs as well.
3) Deceitful / deceptive / underhanded	Ask for material in writing; These folks are often verbally skillful; you need a chance to review in advance and prepare. Seek legal backup.
4) Shrewd / manipulative / exploitative	Provide limits in advance within which this person needs to work.
5) Discourteous / rude / abrasive	Remind this person that courtesy is always appropriate.
6) Egotistical / self-centered / self-seeking	Assign this person tasks which involve helping others
7) Procrastinating / vacillating / delaying	Set specific limits with consequences
8) Rigid / obstinate / unbending	Provide alternatives from which they can choose.
9) Tight-lipped / taciturn / uncommunicative	Invite them to share; assign them jobs which require oral participation
10) Complaining / critical / fault-finding	Ask them to be the "Angel's Advocate (taking the positive side of a point for a change).

Figure 5

Conclusion

Any or all of these ten problematic categories destroy dignity and create negative "psychic income" at the workplace. Managers need to be sure they are working with the problem, and not part of the problem. And of course, the very first area of dignity impairment that Dodson mentions is abusive managers. Both Bramson and Solomon attend to the problematic manager. When I ask my social work students "Who has had a bad manager or supervisor?" everyone raises their hands; many raise two hands! Moreover, they do not raise them slowly either; the hands just shoot right up! So, managers, the first thing we need to do is follow the dictum of the medical profession, "First, do no harm!"

[1]Benedict Carey (2004: p.D1) writes, in the Wall Street Journal about "Fear in the Workplace: The Bullying Boss: Researchers Move from the Playground to the Workplace."
[2]I have added some suggestions about dealing with these types of people.

Part 2 - Chapter 2

THREE (OR FIVE) SEPARATE PARTS CALLED "OUR ORGANIZATION"

Introduction

Organizations are a social reality "sui generis." This Latin phrase means "of itself" and points us to an important reality about organizations. Organizations have a character, a culture, a style, if you will. Orchestras perform in certain distinct ways, even though players, conductors, and the music differ. Restaurants seem to do certain foods well and others not so well. We come to know that, if we want a steak, we go to this place; fish, we go to that place, though each establishment serves both items. Social Agencies have a certain style and approach, whether it is a family service agency, a fund raising agency, a counseling agency, a nursing home, or whatever. Organizations enact and reproduce their skills. Consider the following experiment as an illustration of this:

> Four chimps were put into a cage with a large bunch of bananas hanging from the top of the cage. A pole rose from the bottom of the cage to the banana bunch. One of the chimps immediately began climbing the pole to retrieve the food. As he neared the top a jet of ice water shot out at him. He tried a couple more times with the same result. He soon gave up seeking the bananas. Others intermittently tried it with the same result. Soon none of them bothered about the bananas any more. Then one chimp was removed and a "naive" chimp introduced. He immediately started up the pole, but was pulled back by the other chimps. After a few more tries and a few restraints, he gave up. Over the course of the next weeks the remaining three were swapped out for new chimps. By the end none of the original chimps were there, and none of them tried to get the bananas. And none of them probably knew why.

Now that is organization! Sometimes what we produce and reproduce in organizations is excellent – quality outcomes, quality meals, quality performances of orchestra scores. Sometimes it is not so good. But it does have a life of its own. And it is in this context, that managers work. Indeed, managers are important instruments in organizational reproduction, and as such must take their "teacher" jobs very seriously. Most frequently, when we think of an organization we think of the entire organization as a structural and functional unit. We need to be aware of the whole organization, of course, but the whole organization is comprised of levels and parts that are as important as the whole. In some important ways organizational levels and parts are even more important than the whole, because different protocols and competencies might be required in these different parts, a reality obscured by the fact that we typically refer to organizations as a whole. When we think of a restaurant we think of, well, the restaurant. We do not typically think of the kitchen, the wine cellar, the waiter staff, and the management as distinct parts of the restaurant (though food critics surely do, and food magazines do as well). Three organizational thinkers – Talcott Parsons, Henry Mintzberg and Tom Peters have given us very useful perspectives on organizational parts and elements that are extremely helpful to managers and supervisors. Parsons talks about the levels of organizations (Parsons, 1960), Mintzberg talks about the parts of the organizations (Minztberg, 1989), and Peters talks about changes in organizational dynamics and presentation to cope with more fluid (global, ever-changing) and speedier (web year) pressures (Peters & Waterman, 1982).

The Three-Part View of Talcott Parsons (As Amended)

In an essay written many years ago, the sociologist Talcott Parsons introduced the idea of the three-part organization. His work was off-puttingly called "Some Ingredients of a General Theory of Formal Organization" (Parsons, 1960). Parsons argued that there were three levels within each organization: technical, managerial, and institutional.[1] A study of Parsons suggests that we all might be better served with four system levels. Therefore I am splitting the institutional level into the executive level and the regulatory level.

1. The Technical Level

The technical level actually does the "work" of the organization. This level includes the caseworkers, cooks and waiters, musicians, teachers, professors, beat cops, etc. These people are sometimes called "front room" folks, and serve as the denominator of the "back room/front room" ratio, or the number of support people per worker needed by an organization. Key competencies here are substantive skills in actually doing the work of the organization.

2. The Managerial Level

The next level is the managerial level. For Parsons, the two essential managerial functions are to mediate between the technical organization and personnel and its customers (clients, students, and audience) and to provide the resources necessary to do the actual job (money, space, etc.) (Parsons, 1960).

3. The Institutional Level

Parsons third system level is the institutional level. That would contain, in today's parlance, the CEO and top team on the organizational side and the board of directors and other regulatory bodies that control, direct and impact the organization. A problem is that the top team or Executive level interacts as overall "managers" (sometimes called senior managers) and the boards and regulatory elements exert overall control and direction of the organization. Let's consider each separately as explained under 3A and 3B.

3A. The Executive Level

The third level, for us, then, becomes the Executive level. It contains the CEO (Chief Executive Officer), COO (Chief Operating Officer), CFO (Chief Financial Officer), CIO (Chief Information Officer), CHRO (Chief Human Resources Officer), and any other Chiefs that form the Cabinet, Executive Committee, or top operating group. They function at the "neck" of the hourglass - with the organization spreading out below them and the larger community and society spreading out above them. Their job is to provide leadership so that mission, vision, and values are directed below in terms of guidance, and above, in terms of motivation to provide support and resources.

3B. The Regulatory Level

The next level is the regulatory level. The board of directors fits this level. It contains other bodies and organizations which can control or impact the organization. An accrediting body would be one such organization. Governmental bureaus might be another. The press and other media would be here as well.

A couple things become very clear in this four-part organizational schema. The first is that the organization has a "fuzzy" bottom (customers, consumers, clients, etc) and a "fuzzy" top (regulatory and impactful bodies). This is a point that Tom Peters (Peters & Waterman, 1982) makes in Figure 6 on page 28.

A second is that the constellation of competencies between any two system levels is decidedly different. That is, as you rise within a system level, you become better at the core competency of that level. However, at the "top" of the level, you cross a boundary into a new regime and a new set of core competencies. Older competencies are retained as perspective, rather than as operational elements. If a physician (technical level) becomes a managerial "Doc," then patient care is minimal and managerial tasks take precedence. A similar situation exists when a teacher becomes a principal. Change within a level is transactional change (improvement) within the system; change between levels is transformational or a change of the system.

In that sense the organization is not really one thing, but, rather, four organizations stacked on top of one another. This four-in-one concept might be hard to grasp, but it is worth spending some time on. Managers especially have their own system level, with their own tasks and functions. And Mintzberg gives us yet more complexity.

An Archetype of a Traditional Organizational Structure

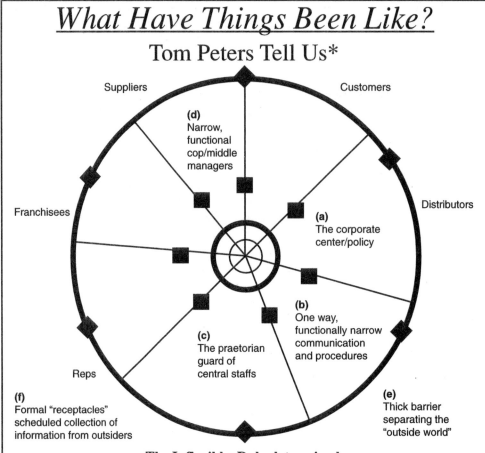

What Have Things Been Like?

Tom Peters Tell Us*

Suppliers

Customers

(d)
Narrow,
functional
cop/middle
managers

(a)
The corporate
center/policy

Franchisees

Distributors

(b)
One way,
functionally narrow
communication
and procedures

(c)
The praetorian
guard of
central staffs

Reps

(f)
Formal "receptacles"
scheduled collection of
information from outsiders

(e)
Thick barrier
separating the
"outside world"

**The Inflexible, Rule-determined,
Mass Producer of the Past: All Persons Know Their Place**

Start with (a), the corporate center / policy. This is the traditional, invisible, impersonal, generally out-of-touch corporate hub. The tininess of the circle representing the corporate center suggests both tightness and narrowness of scope; communication to the outside world (in or beyond the firm's official boundary) is usually via formal declaration -- the policy manual or the multivolume plan, by and large determined on high - and communicated via the chain of command (i.e., downward). Within this tiny circle lie the "grains of the organization." It is here, almost exclusively, that the long-term thinking, planning, and peering into the future take place.

Tom Peters, "Restoring American Competitiveness: Looking for New Models of Organizations." Academy of Management Executives, 2, 2 (May 1988): 103-107.

Figure 6

The Six-Part View of Henry Mintzberg (As Amended)

Perhaps a better way for you to think about Mintzberg's (1989) work is 5 + 1. The five parts of the organization are outlined in Figure 7, with the entire organization contained or bound by ideology or values. The central "stack" as it were has three parts, similar to that of Parsons. At the bottom is the "operating core" (the technical system in Parsons' terms). In the middle is, you guessed it, the "middle line." That would be Parsons' managerial level. Finally, at the top there is the "strategic apex." This level would correspond to the executive level in my reformulation of Parsons.

Mintzberg's Five Parts of the Organization*
(See http://list-socrates-berkley.edu/ufmb/articles/mmt3hera)

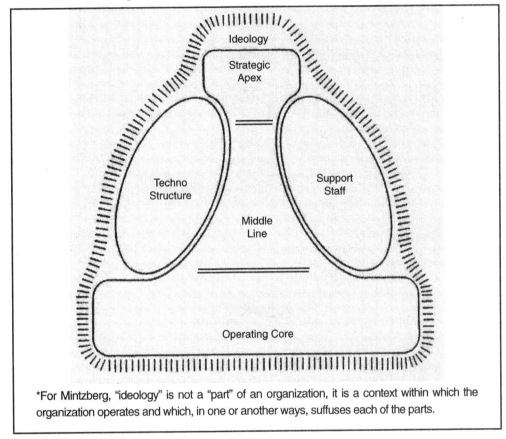

*For Mintzberg, "ideology" is not a "part" of an organization, it is a context within which the organization operates and which, in one or another ways, suffuses each of the parts.

Figure 7

Mintzberg adds two sidebars that stand as giant eggs on either side of the stack. One is the techno structure, and the other is the support staff. Readers will note there are spaces between the two eggs and the rest of the organization, suggesting (correctly) that while part of the same package they have a certain degree of organizational independence. That is why I added the two sets of double lines between operating core and middle line, and between the middle line and the strategic apex. Mintzberg did not have that separation in his original diagram but it makes sense and follows the lead that he suggested in the separation of techno structure and support staff. What Mintzberg calls "ideology" we might call culture or values. Ideology is in the ballpark but a little strong.

Tom Peters' Newer and Older Models of Organizations

Tom Peters is one of the most fertile thinkers about organizations today. The fact that he is not an academic like Parsons and Mintzberg works, I think, in his favor. Like Parsons, Peters is interested in the way an organization responds to its environment. Like Mintzberg, he sees the organization as "encapsulated" – more so in the older model he describes than the newer one.

An Archtype of a Contemporary Organization

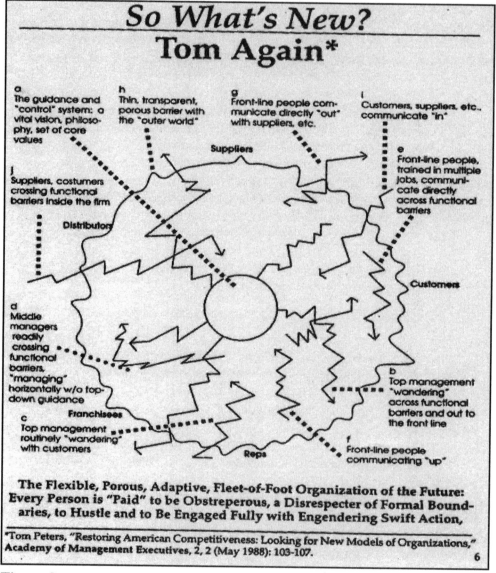

Figure 8

In Figures 6 (page 28) and 8 (page 30), Peters describes the older and the newer models of organization (Peters & Waterman, 1982). In the "Inflexible, Rule Determined Mass Producer of the Past" there is a thick boundary separating the internal organization and the outside organization. It was hard to get in, but once you were in you were, well, "in". This might be a combination of Quinn's Clan and Hierarchy models, which was discussed earlier in Part 2 (Quinn, 1988). Insulation continues into the very center of the organization. The executive core is exceptionally well insulated, and thus a great distance from the customers and the controllers mentioned by Parsons. If "uncertainty absorption" exists in any organization it is here, because information is very "processed" by the time it gets to the boss.

The newer organizational model that Peters described is a nimble, open model. The thinness of the lines suggests the permeability of the boundary. Indeed it is difficult to be sure who is or is not a "member" of the organization, because those with various kinds of relationships to it (customers and suppliers are seen inside the organization, and employees are "outside" of it working with customers and consumers). It is the boundryless organization, something of a combo between Quinn's Adhocracy and Market models.

Peters' diagrams in essence refer to the "whole" organization, and they are useful in that way. While none of us organizationally might be exactly either one of them, we could locate ourselves in an organizational "space" defined by his dimensions. If we use his dimensions, we have a table something like the one in Figure 9. It might be fun to locate your organization in that space. The table assumes that all organizations have properties of the variables suggested by Peters, rather than being one or the other.

An Organizational "Space" Defined by Porosity and Rigidity

Rigid ╲ Porous	Low	High
Low	Low Porosity/Low Rigidity Ex: a Flexible Tube	High Porosity/Low Rigidity Ex: an Amoeba
High	Low Porosity/High Rigidity Rigidity Ex: a Steel Box	High Porosity/High Rigidity Ex: a Colander

Figure 9

The Organizational Circle

Peters' illustrations are evocative in another way. Most of the time organizations are rendered in the box and line mode known as the "organization chart" (see Figure 10). So common is this rendering that we barely need to illustrate it. It has become the definition of hierarchical authority, of who is "over" whom and who "reports to" whom. Because it is in level mode, meeting with someone who is not your supervisor or manager, but who is "over" them, becomes a "skip level" meeting and causes, usually, all kinds of issues.

A Traditional Organization Chart

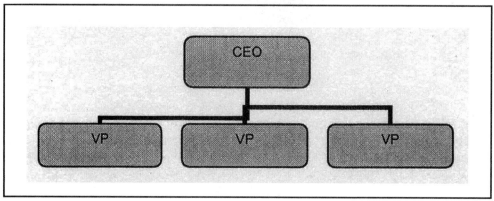

Figure 10

The circles Peters' uses invite us to think of other ways to render organizational relationships, ways that have inherent order and regularity in them and to them. Thinking about the organization as a solar system or as an atom has some value (Tropman, 1989). Notice that in this rendering (see Figure 11), departments orbit the Executive, rather than being beneath them. The executive then becomes "central" to the departments, rather than "over" them, an important difference, the full implications of which change the very nature of organization relationships. The solar system model (Figure 11A) also means that only "orbits" not "levels" are crossed, giving the Executive better access to all parts of the organization. It also suggests dynamism and changing of positions, rather than stasis.

Note that in the atom rendition (Figure 11B), the orbits are elliptical. This is an important addition. It means that departments have positions both close to and far from the executive core. Such variability is really a good thing. If a department becomes too close to the executive core it can become co-opted by that view. On the other hand, if a department is too far from the center of the organization the executive core loses awareness and supportive views. Hence a "now-closer-now-further" dynamic can work very well.

The Organization as a Solar System or an Atom

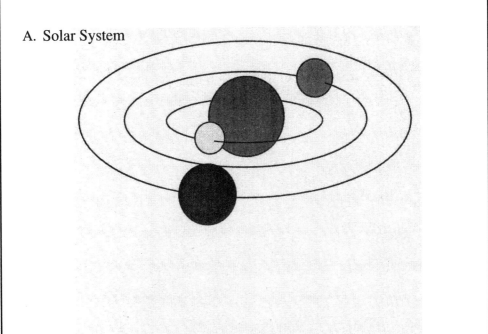

A. Solar System

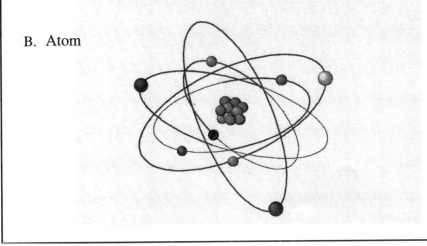

B. Atom

Figure 11

There are other ways to think about organizations as well. One CEO, with whom I talked, argued for the "Pizza" model (Figure 12), an application which was quite innovative. In the "Pizza" model, underlying everything is "dough." Given the importance of money to organizations, that is not so far fetched. Thin crust, thick crust, each refers to the richness of the resources that the organization can access. Over the crust is, well, "the big cheese." Then we have big pepperonis, little pepperonis, olives, mushrooms, or whatever, all as parts of the organizational pizza. In a funny way, it works.

The Organization as a Pizza

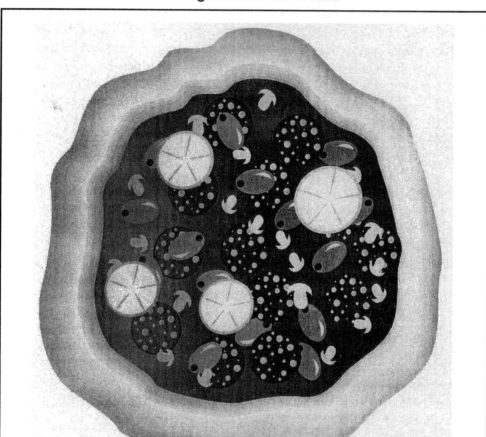

Figure 12

Readers may find these metaphors a bit of a stretch. but I hope you will not dismiss them out of hand and instead give it some thought. You can even play with them a bit. It might be fun at a staff meeting to see if teams of staff could actually draw the agency as a circle, or an atom, or a pizza. Then think about how relationships might change as a result.

Organizations as a Matrix of Permission and Control

Organizations are most often seen as control structures. A lot of what organizations actually do is designed to emphasize this aspect of their functioning. "Reporting Relationships," "lines of authority," and other such concepts stress the function of control. Indeed, conventional understanding of the very aspect of "managing" and "supervising" contains the subtext of "bossing." And the boss, of course, is someone with more power who controls you, softly or sternly. The sociological literature is full of books and courses on social control, the larger framework of organizational control.

Managers not only control, they also permit. Hence, you might think as I do, that the emphasis on social control has been an overemphasis, to the extent that it ignores social permission, or the "okaying" of a whole range of behavioral repertoires. Some simple examples might be the using of office supplies for personal purposes. Some organizations are tight with this; others loose. Padding expense accounts, nepotistic hiring (and lack of firing), sexual relationships in or related to the workplace, are but a few examples of the kinds of things that organizations support for us and teach us how to do. Often, formally, the very same organization would deny any connection with such practices. But then, they are in the informal system and the culture, so that there is lots of deniability available.

Managers need to be aware that organizations supply permissions and controls. To see only part of the picture is to miss the full richness of the organization. You can say the same, of course, for families, communities and societies. We all exist in a "permission/control space" in which our environment arranges for supplies of permissions as well as supplies of controls (Tropman, 1986). Consider the following "permission/control space" as described in Figure 13.

Organizations as a Function of Supplies of Permission / Control

Control	Permission	
	Low	**High**
Low	Low Permission/Low Control Ex: a Volunteer Organization	High Permission/Low Control Ex: a Start-up Agency
High	Low Permission/High Control Ex: a Public Child Welfare Agency	High Permission/High Control Ex: a State Disaster Relief Organization

Figure 13

The literature on management is curiously bifurcated. On the one hand, it is written, first, as if people did not matter. The "scientific management" approach tended to see people as replaceable parts (http://www.accel-team.com/scientific/scientific_02.htm). Whatever humanness they had was irrelevant to their functioning in the organization. "Our way or the highway" was a suitable mantra. Span of control was a key element - span being the number of people you could actually observe and check. That number was, well, five. Given the importance of the span of control concept, it is no wonder that organizations grew tall and pointy. Everyone was managing/supervising five direct reports.

As the "human factor" came into more prominence, mostly after 1945, people (as people) became more important. Personnel departments morphed into Human Resources departments. Human factors became specifically important as "the greatest resource" of an organization. Span of control became span of communication. In this span of communication, supervisors and managers could oversee many more than 5 people because they did not have to check the work of each person; that person checked their own work and came to the supervisor for help if and as needed. The magical 5 became 50. You could supervise 5 within the span of control but, you could resource 50 in the shift to a span of communication.

Of course, as span of control became span of communication, organizational direction moved from external to internal, span of permission increased also. These changes required not only technical skills on the part of the worker, but judgment as well. Criteria became vaguer, and simultaneous mutual feedback, sort of like what happens in driving, became the norm.[2] The job of the manager changed from overseer to guide, to some extent, but the jobs changed faster, generally, than the managers did.

For the reasons just mentioned, communication, interpersonal skills, and group process skills became more important. Most seemed to agree that managers needed these skills, but it was somewhat unclear exactly what actually were "good" communication, interpersonal skills, and group process skills. Certainly, there are technical elements to each, such as effective listening, clear use of language, communication using more than one medium (speaking and writing, for example, or speaking and having video or audio backup). Seminars in "supportive communication," "active listening," and tests on "communication styles" are now a mainstay of managerial training at most executive education centers.

Emotional Management in the Workplace

What took a lot longer to develop was the recognition that part of the humanness that employees brought to their workplace was their emotions. Getting people into the workplace did not automatically bring feelings into the workplace. The pioneer in this work was Arlie Russell Hochschild. According to Bianchi (2004), Hochschild's framework involves three elements:

1. The culture of emotional display rules,
2. Surface and deep emotion,
3. Emotion, work and management.

It is this last piece - emotion work and management - that is of special interest here, in particular, her book "The Managed Heart," is a landmark in this approach (Hochschild, 1983; 2003). She specifically studies flight attendants and their job which was essentially to manage hostiles. Hostiles are passengers who are angry, cannot get off the plane (it is in the air!) and may well have had too much to drink. She explains how flight attendants learn to manage feelings in situations such as this. In the process she accomplished a much larger task, pointing out that the workplace is a sea of emotions and feelings, and that organizations have developed ways (largely unacknowledged, and largely done by women) to "manage" (address, respond, accommodate to) these feelings.

Conventionally, of course, we are all aware of the employee to whom others confide, who arranges monthly birthday celebrations, who tries to make the workplace a colorful and pleasant place to work visually and attitudinally. But until recently these tasks were considered sidebars, nice add-ons to the "real" job of whatever the job description said, and it certainly did not include being nice to people and bringing flowers to the office. Managers must now recognize that "managing" feelings and emotions are a core part of the managerial task, and I mean that in the very best sense. Managing in this context means recognizing the emotionality of situations, responding appropriately to the expressing of feeling, encouraging and channeling appropriate feeling into constructive pathways, and dealing, especially with anger, your own and that of others. These latter two are known as "affect control."

A few years after The Managed Heart was written, a tool came along to provide concrete assistance in the effort to understand emotional management in the workplace called Emotional Intelligence. Daniel Goleman wrote Emotional Intelligence in 1995. The "EQ" was seen as even more important than the "IQ" in understanding success and failure in organizations. This concept deals with self-awareness, feeling management, motivation, empathy, and social skills. Self-awareness is knowing what you feel when you feel it. Management of feelings is the ability to control impulses, soothe your anxiety and have appropriate anger. Motivation, in the EQ framework, involves zeal, persistence and optimism in the face of setbacks. Empathy is the ability to respond and read unspoken feelings. Finally, social skills require the ability to handle the emotional reactions of others, interacting, smoothing, and managing relationships. (See Figure 20, p. 64)

Conclusion

Looking at the three models presented here, and connecting them back to those of Robert Quinn mentioned earlier, managers can see that their "managerial work" is likely to be heavily influenced by the setting in which they work. Several important insights come from their work, which I would like to review and is as follows:

One is that the organization, overall, does have identifiable structural and cultural features. Quinn is good here in alerting us to the clan, bureaucracy, market, and adhocracy cultures (Quinn, 1988). While there are of course other organizational typologies, Quinn's is both instructive in and of itself, and as a sensitizing device, to all of us in agencies, to look around and see what kind of place is it in which we are working. While many aspects of management and supervision are common across all venues, there are differences in the pace, expectations, demand schedule, and outcome measures that managerial supervisors must take into account.

This might be a good time for readers to take a moment and get a sheet of paper. Put My Organization at the top. Identify your organization's primary features (use Quinn if you like, or anything else that makes sense to you) on the left hand side of the page. Then, on the right hand side, list the elements which you as a manager/supervisor need to take especially into account given the nature of your organization. Here is an example:

My Organization	Special Supervisory Requirements
Ex: Clinical Agency Ex: Child Protective Service	Ex: Knowledge of Clinical Method Ex: Child Safety Issues; Federal and State Law

The work of Tom Peters also points to the "fuzzy" nature of contemporary organizations (Peters & Waterman, 1982). All of them may not be as open as suggested in his second diagram, but we all fit somewhere in a space described by his two variables.

Secondly, the work of Parsons, points us to the "fuzzy" edges of the organization - both at the input and output sides/edges where clients, consumers, customers, vendors, and others influence us (Parsons, 1960). Managers often have contact with the outside, and need to keep their requirements and demands always in their minds. Part of managements' task is to help clarify and structure, and then reclarify and restructure these "fuzzy" relationships. Then too, Parsons points to the "control" elements - the board and other administrative bodies that have fateful relations with the organization. These are "fuzzy" as well. He also points to the "independence" of the organizational "parts" at least to a degree. Hence, as managers move into management from "worker" or "technical system" status, they are moving to a job with as many differences as if they had actually moved to another agency. Mintzberg stresses the uniqueness and autonomy of the organizational parts as well (Mintzberg, 1989). Though he does have the whole organization surrounded by a net of "ideology" (more fuzziness) his central insight about intraorganizational uniqueness remains robust.

The work I did on the organizational circle and other ways of conceptualizing and displaying organizations is useful both directly, as another way to draw your organization, and as a thought experiment - another way to think about your organization.

The work on emotions in the workplace and the need for emotional management as an important part of the manager's toolkit opens new doors for competency development. Understanding that emotion work is part of the regular work that organizations do challenges managers to take a new view of their job.

The discussions in this chapter refer to all organizations. However, nonprofits have some special issues and challenges themselves. Let us move, now, to looking at nonprofits specifically.

---

[1] I do not recommend one actually read the late Professor Parsons. His prose is thick and often lacks crispness. A good way to think about it might be that he thinks in German and writes in English. That said, his ideas are great.

[2] In driving a car, every driver is in a process of simultaneous mutual adjustment, based upon the constant inflow and outflow of informaton.

Part 2 - Chapter 3

NONPROFIT AND HUMAN SERVICE ORGANIZATIONS[1]

Introduction

As organizations go, they have much in common. The three largest classes commonly discussed are corporate organizations, governmental organizations, and nonprofit organizations. Most of us have a common sense of the differences, and tend to think of them as rather different buckets (or you could use boxes, separate bundles, etc.) of structures and functions. The fact of the matter is that these organizational "types" are much less distinct than you might think, or what may have been true in the past. For one thing, within each sector there are very large and very small organizations.

The University of Michigan is a nonprofit organization, and it has a budget of 4+ billion dollars and change. Some storefront nonprofits have only one employee, and many community organizations have no employees at all, operating just on volunteer time and energy. The same scope can be found in the corporate sector, from large publicly traded companies like General Electric (and private companies like Cargill) to small "Mom and Pop" organizations and sole proprietorships. Governmental organizations run from EXOP (The Executive Office of the President of the United States) to small county and city operations. Then there are school districts, water districts, library districts, mental health catchment areas, and so on. In terms of size then, each sector runs the gamut. There may be more in common among similar sized organization across sectors than within sector.

In terms of function, I can make a similar point. Almost nothing is the purview on one sector anymore. Consider national defense or police, typically a governmental function, we now have Blackwater USA working in Iraq, and also private police and prison systems there. Blackwater USA is comprised of five companies: Blackwater Training Center, Blackwater Target Systems, Blackwater Security Consulting, Blackwater Canine, and Blackwater Air (AWS). According to their website, www.blackwaterusa.com, they "have established a global presence and provide training and tactical solutions for the 21st century." We have private prisons in the US as well. Child care involves elements of all three sectors. Gerontological care, health care, substance abuse, and counseling - all of these fields have corporate, governmental and nonprofit entities working in them. We will look at the nonprofit sector specifically in Chapter 4. These commonalities make the manager's job a puzzlement. Does it really matter where you run a child care center?

One kind of difference is within each sector. Corporations, nonprofits, and governmental bureaus range from large to small and vary on many other dimensions as well (product, purpose, history, etc. etc.). There is a lot of intrasector difference, which makes looking at intersector difference all the more difficult. These differences within the sector also add managerial complications. Running a somewhat big (say $100 million) organization in any one sector may have lots in common with running big organizations in the other two sectors.

However, there are some unique features to nonprofits, both in characteristics and problems, though these problems may be found in other sectors as well. Peter Frumkin, in his book "On Being Nonprofit" (2002), argues as follows:

> Attempting to define the fundamental features of the disparate entities that constitute the nonprofit and voluntary sector is a daunting task. Yet there are at least three features that connect these widely divergent (divergent according to Frumkin, JET) entities: (1) they do not coerce participation; (2) they operate without distributing their profits to shareholders; and (3) they exist without simple and clear lines of ownership and accountability. (Frumkin, 2002. p. 3)

I agree with Frumkin that there are those differences, although I am not convinced about the "coercion" element. It seems, except for volunteers themselves, to be similar among the three major types of organizations. Frumkin does not mention, specifically, the differing legal status that the organizations have, and that we as citizens provide a tax expenditure (in terms of tax forgiveness) for the nonprofit organization. Nor, does he stress the fact that the expectations around nonprofit employment, for better behavior of employees – including managers and executives – and less compensation ("you do not go into nonprofit work to get rich," is a common mantra) are issues with which the nonprofit manager must deal. From a managerial standpoint, however, there are a number of stresses and pressures the nonprofit world faces which, while probably not completely unique, are sufficiently prominent to deserve mention. They will be the subject matter of this chapter, because they represent pressing, if not unique, challenges with which the nonprofit manager must cope.

In social work we face the continuously stressful press of human problems, the lack of needed resources, and the constant worry about how much and what kind of help is appropriate. You would think that these pressures would make outstanding management a priority, and that management would try to create work settings that avoid burnout. On the contrary, we create caseloads that increase it. You would think we would create a management, which would shepherd and increase resources. On the contrary, we exploit our own staff and whine "poor boy" rhetoric. The facts of the matter are that social work agencies are under managed and under led. I do not mean, by this observation, that agencies do not have executive directors, CEOs, CPOs (Chief Professional

Officer), associate directors, and so on. There is both the apparatus of administration and the machinery of management. The problem is that, all too often, it does not work very well. (And, I should add in farmers, management and leadership in for profits and government is no model either!)

What Are the Problems Facing Nonprofits?

Worldwide the totals are staggering and what are the remedies considering that the nonprofit sector, in the United States alone, involves well over 750,000 organizations with one or more paid staff, and a sector budget of $750 billion, not counting churches (New York Times, 2/3/00, p. c12). Looking at the sector and understanding it, becomes a crucial step toward excellent management. The missions, especially of the social work/human service organizations are vital. Assisting fellow humans in coping with problems that beset them can be and must be one of the most rewarding experiences in workplace life. Rewarding, that is, if the workplace itself is structured to nourish the work against the inevitable problems and struggles that our fellow persons present, both in terms of individuals whom we have helped, as it were, "to fall off the wagon," and the seemingly endless resupply of problems, like sexual abuse, domestic violence, hunger, child neglect, etc. Working with these problems on a daily basis requires a supportive, nurturing, and well run workplace.

Rather than this, we have a spare, often dismal workplace, under funded and overworked, without fun and spirit, and occasionally, mean spirited. Here are some of the problems, drawn not only from my own observations as I have seen them, but also from countless interviews with nonprofit executives, and many hours of consultation.

Improvements are urgently needed with a Remedies section after each of the problems that addresses the need for change. Let's look at some ideas in the areas I have mentioned. These are ideas that middle managers, project managers, and supervisory managers can begin with. In some cases (for example the board of directors), middle managers, project managers, and supervisory managers cannot and do not have much influence. For good or ill, board relationships are the purview of the CEO/President. But there are other areas where managers can begin the process of improvement.

Here, the middle managers, project managers, and supervisory managers play a supporting and encouraging role. They need to be aware of the need for change, support the Executive Director in this change, and "talking up" and representing the need for change throughout the organization.

It is important to note that in the following sections middle managers, project managers, and supervisory managers cannot do much but support change efforts within their organizations.

Problem: Boards of directors are deeply flawed – they seriously underperform and malperform. Let's start where the buck stops. Nonprofit boards are in need of much (really huge!!) improvement. While for-profit boards have much to answer for, and have been poor performers in many cases, nonprofit boards are, amazingly, even worse. They are worse because, in effect, they have no oversight. They are, in effect, like public servants. Insulated, as both groups are from the "political" process, they are insulated, as well, from accountability and responsibility. No one "fires" a nonprofit director (board member). Many times I have worked with boards which are of illegal compliance, having members sitting for two or three terms past their allowed timeframe (usually a maximum of two terms, or six years) because no one has the courage to tell them to move on.

To this abuse we can add scores of others. For example, board members often have no idea what they are to do individually and collectively; their processes and meetings become a venue for expressing and implementing private agendas; they are typically "run," by the most socially "powerful" person on the board. Status and deference operating as they typically do, other members defer to the socially prominent. Even the best ones fail in many areas and the worst ones are abysmal. They create, as Deming said, "incalculable loss" (Deming, 1982). Among their most egregious failure is setting the direction for the organization and reviewing the executive director. As important as it is, the board does not care about management in the largest, most positive sense, providing vision and strategic guidance for the agency and the executive. This charge may be a bit unfair - board members do not come to their positions as callous individuals. In the absence of knowledge and guidance they resort to their default position, pushing their own agenda. This situation is beginning to change in the US. Board Source (formerly the National Center for Nonprofit Boards) is making important strides by offering consulting and training services for Nonprofit Boards, one-day courses, and a website (www.boardsource.org) that features a question and answer section, a bookstore, and online information on the services and courses they offer.

Remedies: Boards of Directors are deeply flawed. A total overhaul of nonprofit boards is needed. In the US, nonprofits are publicly supported organizations in that they are relieved of taxes. All boards should, therefore, account to the public about the accomplishments and trials of their organizations each year. It should be required that all board members/directors be trained in proper board responsibilities and deportment. The organization is not their plaything. Every board should evaluate itself and each director every year. Each board should have a strategic plan that is posted on its website (of course that means they need a website). There should be job descriptions for each board position, from member through chairperson, to clarify what is expected. And each year every director should be required, as a part of continuation, to undergo one new piece of training.

Problem: The Executive Director/CEO/CPO and the top team are often untrained or maltrained at the front end. Social work executives lack managerial and executive training to help them in their tasks. For one thing, there is little administrative training either in the degree program (MSW curricula), as they are on the way to an executive position (management certificate and post grad programs) or when they are an executive (continuing education programs). There is a bit of a vicious cycle here. It is not available because we cannot afford it. We cannot afford it because the boards do not believe it counts, even though some of the board members have themselves, through their commercial organizations, enjoyed such training. Because the boards do not think it counts, the executives do not either. Because the executives do not, they do not press their boards; you can see where this goes ... nowhere. Hence, executives are, by and large, untrained in management and leadership competencies.

If this situation sounds bad, it is, but unfortunately, it is actually worse. Executives are also maltrained. In the absence of training, executives use the skills of their last position assuming they are appropriate for the new one. Let me explain what I mean by maltrained. Organizations exist in three broad skill bands: the technical band, the managerial band, and the institutional band (Recall Professor Parsons in the last section). This means that there are two kinds of managers in social work agencies, the top team and the top person. What happens frequently is that an excellent technical person or a worker (it could be a teacher, an engineer, a whatever) is, because of that excellence, promoted into the managerial ranks. This promotion is based upon the assumption, held by the promoters and the promotees that the new job is an extension of, rather than different from, the old job. This is a point I mentioned in the previous chapter.

As many organization observers have pointed out, there are qualitative shifts as you cross levels, which require qualitatively different skill sets. In fact, being good at your old job may, in effect, disqualify you for your new job. Why is that? The answer is that whatever we are good at becomes our "default" style. Under stress, which the move to a new job certainly is, we are more likely to resort to that "default" style, other things being equal. That means that the therapist, upon becoming director, "defaults" to therapeutic-style skills and styles as a manager. This is something all of us have seen as social workers. We may even have performed this way ourselves. Indeed, so common is this phenomenon that an early diagnostic version of it emerged as "The Peter Principle." This principle, developed by Lawrence J. Peter, sought to explain why so many managers were incompetent (Peter, 1970 & 1972 and Kane, 1970). He observed that organizations structured incompetence, by promoting employees until they reached their level of incompetence. There they would remain.

Use of the default style is encouraged by more than just stress. Here is where training comes in, or more accurately, does not come in. And here again there is progress. "Nonprofit Management" is a growth area in American Higher Education. Centers around the US (Indiana University, Case Western Reserve University, and others) are under vigorous development. But the need is still great.

Remedies: The Executive Director/CEO/CPO & the top team are often untrained or maltrained at the front end. Requirements that managerial training be part of a candidate's portfolio, as well as "experience" should be part of every search process. Let's step up to the plate and begin a process that requires training of executives and top team members.

Problem: The Executive Director/CEO/CPO & the top team are cast adrift. Because of the board problems and the training problems just mentioned, the Executive Director/CEO/CPO and the top team are in many ways left to "twist slowly in the wind". This point connects, of course, to the board, which is supposed to provide policy direction, on the one hand, and executive appraisal, on the other, but which rarely does either. Executives are surrounded by high and often unexpressed expectations. Praise is meager; criticism voluminous. Here again, progress is on the horizon. For example,

The Amherst Wilder Foundation in Minneapolis has taken a leadership role in making "easy to use materials" available to executives and their staffs in a variety of key areas.[3]

Remedies: The Executive Director/CEO/CPO & the top team are cast adrift. The strategic plan should provide the basis for the annual plan that the Executive Director/CEO/CPO carries out. It should be the responsibility of the executive committee to see that such a plan is in place, and that it is connected to the evaluation of the Executive Director/CEO/CPO.

Problem: Continuing education programs for social work managers & executives are few. Given the large number of nonprofit human service organizations, you would expect a flourishing industry of post degree training and education programs. If the front end training is thin, perhaps, once on the job, managers and executives could build skills with a seminar here, a workshop there, over the course of their careers. Sadly, this is not the case. The "big" systems - the United Way of America, the Girl Scouts, the Child Welfare League of America, and so on have executive training programs for their executives. These are, of course, to be encouraged and expanded. But outside of this effort, social work managers and executives find it difficult to find programs, and to pay for them when they do find programs. For example, Carnegie Mellon University in Pittsburgh, as recently as January of 2000, had to postpone a training program it was planning for nonprofit executives in the Pittsburgh area because support "dried up" and the executives and their agencies could not (or would not) assume the full (and modest) cost. This kind of situation is another way in which managers are left adrift.

Remedies: Continuing education programs for social work managers & executives are few. Executives need to develop a career path for themselves, and need assistance in doing so. As part of this career pathing, executive and top team training, AFTER hire and DURING tenure, should be a no-brainer. It should be present, just as board training is present. If the organization does not provide continuing educational opportunities it is worthwhile for middle managers, project managers, and supervisory managers to seek out opportunities on their own.

Problem: The Managerial Mindset is underrepresented in the Social Work culture. Social work seems to be focused on helping people (individuals and families) with problems or reshaping social policy. Somehow, and I have heard this hundreds of times, "managing" does not seem like a social work task. Social workers feel it is inappropriate to express a desire to be an executive. All too frequently, social work executives comment, as do Deans in academia, that they have been "sentenced" to a management position. The idea seems to be that, because our hearts are pure and our intentions good, "management" is somehow not needed. Somehow, many social workers apparently feel good intentions are enough. They forget, of course, that the road to hell is paved with good intentions. Very little, from families to pickup games to organizations, is self managed over the long haul. Management, of course, is the art of getting work done through others. Somehow, in social work, this does not seem like the real work of helping. This has the same invalidity as arguing that mothers do not know anything about managing because they have been "at home." The utter nonsense of a claim, however, not only does little to detract from its acceptance, but in many instances seems to become paradoxically supportive of its validity.

Yet there is a counter text to the negative orientation to the managerial mindset. Even though management is unappreciated or underappreciated, and even though there is a naive faith in the power of good intentions to somehow self organize, the social worker on the ground experiences and feels the effects of bad management. Hundreds of social workers with whom I have talked complain that their social agency is badly run...and then they go on to give chilling example after chilling example. Some how, and this is paradoxical to me, the "felt problems" of bad management have not translated into support for good management.

Remedies: The managerial mindset is underrepresented in the social work culture. In each community there should be an informal organization of human service executives in social work as well as governmental managers. They should beat the drum about the importance of good management. This can be done at Rotary/Kiwanis/Lions meetings, public symposia, and local schools and colleges, or anyplace anyplace that will listen. I am especially thinking of social work gatherings. We need to change the prevailing mindset.

Problem: The human resources function is undeveloped. Not only is the management function underrated, the worker function is underrated. Oddly, for an agency dealing with helping people, the typical social work agency has underdeveloped human resources function aimed at helping few workers. I think perhaps the volunteer tradition that started our field and that continues to this day may have something to do with the under appreciation of the social worker themselves. The "volunteer" versus "the professional" is a war that has not yet been worked through. On the other hand, there is a vigorous subtext that "anyone can do it." This subtext receives sustenance from the long tradition of volunteerism in social work. When I ask workers who report the awful stories mentioned above "Why do you stay?" They reply that they like helping and they like their coworkers. And, they often add, bad as the management is, "I can live with it." Part of this problem stems from a lack of board and executive knowledge about the importance of human resource management. Part stems from a curious undervaluing of the importance of professional social work itself. On the one hand we talk about the importance of professional training, but on the other we neglect executives and workers by providing little means to access professional training.

Remedies: The human resources function is undeveloped. Agencies need to develop their human resources function. Each agency should have a human resources manager and it is not necessary that this person be a full time person. Rather, several agencies could share this person, thus cutting cost. We need to stop the process of underpaying staff and then guilt tripping them into a program of self-exploitation as it is unseemly, and sends exactly the wrong message.

Problem: Fiscal knowledge is limited. The limited training executives and future executives do receive, for executive and managerial roles, is very shy on financial management skills, including accounting. While no respectable training course in research would omit a statistics course, most social work management training programs (including The University of Michigan's) do not include an accounting course. We do have a course in budgeting, but that is not always offered. Such continuing education programs that do exist are frequently thin on the financial aspects. Also, there is little encouragement of executives, by boards, to gain more fiscal knowledge. At the Executive Education Center at the University of Michigan, for example, there is a seminar on "Financial Management for the Non Financial Manager." There is rarely a nonprofit executive in attendance.

Remedies: Fiscal knowledge is limited. Regular training in fiscal management is needed for nonprofit staff and managers. In Detroit, MI, there is an organization called the Accounting Aid Society (not the best name perhaps but really the best idea) (accountingaidsare4u.org). It began helping organizations in fiscal areas, and now provides a range of training opportunities for nonprofit staff in fiscal and other areas. Every town should have an organization like this with such a function.

Problem: Technological development is lagging. What is true for financial management is also true for technology. Nonprofits are twentieth century at best. Computer based applications, email, and web based activities are a long way from standard at most social service agencies. Equipment is often second or third generation, technology knowledge limited, and technology based activities the subject of a running series of jokes about "the computer this" and "the computer that."

Remedies: Technological development is lagging. The same point I made about fiscal applies to electronic and computer based technology. Running on old or discarded equipment is not acceptable. The case needs to be made for current equipment. If necessary, dollars need to be raised for this. Standards of computer literacy should be established and enforced throughout each agency, beginning with the top. Recently, I was trying to get in touch with a nonprofit executive of great reputation and fulsome resource who was "on travel." This nonprofit executive does not "do" email or carry a cell phone, his secretary does his e-mail and snail mails it to him. How can we expect agencies to forge ahead when the boss is way behind?

Problem: The voice of the customer (consumer, client) is largely silent. For some reason social work has never embraced the program and services assessment mindset either (Could it be because our clients were poor and it did not matter?). Executives, all too often, become apologists for lackluster agency performance rather than leaders down the road of better quality. Quality is driven by feedback, feedback from the user. Regretfully, we have not as yet put evaluation systems in place. I stress these systems because such systems, as well as managers, can help employees improve performance.

Remedies: The voice of the customer (consumer, client) is largely silent. Each agency needs to develop its own set of internal and external customers and ask them for feedback, often, and in detail. In America, most car dealerships (known to be among the lowest in customer service) at least give customers a card to mail in rating the service. Most human service organizations do not meet even this minimal standard.

Problem: Evaluation is largely process based rather than results based. Connected with the issue of "customer" evaluation is the issue of the results of human intervention. Are we, at the end of the day, adding value, helping people, and/or making a difference? Famous wit Dorothy Parker's comment applies here as well. When told that the American President Calvin Coolidge had died, she is supposed to have asked "How can they tell?" This question applies to nonprofit human service organizations specifically. "Are you helping?" "And how can you tell?" Doing "good" is not enough. You need to do it right, and do it well! Such evaluations procedures, as are largely in place, tend to be of a process nature - we "saw" so many clients, we have so many children in our center, etc. But does anyone get better? On THAT question we often have little to share. Not all process measures are problematic - hot meals served, women given shelter, etc. are some examples of acceptable. But overall, evaluation needs to be drastically improved.

Remedies: Evaluation is largely process based rather than results based. Agencies must be open to the question "Do we make a difference?" And, if the answer is "NO", change. If the answer is "YES," then a second question must be asked, "Does the difference we make matter?" And for both inquiries, the further questions of "How do we know that?" and "Is our information reliable and valid?" need to be satisfactorily addressed.

In some areas (Members of the Child Welfare League of America for example) there is a process of accreditation. We should consider this for human service agencies across the board, except not exactly as a form of accreditation. Rather, I am thinking that all agencies should be rated, locally, like restaurants and wines. Local papers usually have a food editor, and now they could have a nonprofit editor. This individual could anonymously sample the wares of a variety of agencies and write about them in the paper. This approach, I think, is the only approach (the glare of getting a 7.5 out of 10 on the nonprofit guide and having this available to the general public) that will get agencies off their duffs. Readers will skim what I have written and say "Hmm, sounds ok, I'll look into it." And that will be the end. Regretful as it is, negative publicity is one big motivator in today's world. Each town would have two guides. One is the Nonprofit organization guide, just mentioned.

The second is the Nonprofit executive guide. This would be like the kind of thing that is written up about sports figures. Who is this person, what have they accomplished, what trouble have they been in (or not), what do people think, etc.? Chefs have it; artists have it, even professors have it (on University websites, Ratemyrprofessor.com). It is time for nonprofit execs to be subject to such public review. Let us recognize the truly great individuals that do run outstanding agencies; let's also criticize boards that terminate outstanding executives because of small-minded chairpersons. But let us also cite executives who have consistent problems. And let us expose agencies which should actually die and help them along.

Problem: Consultative help is not available or is episodic. Commercial organizations have troubles too. But they can call upon Bain & Co, or McKinsey or any number of other famous consulting firms to send in teams to help them out. This function is largely absent in the human service community. There are, of course, individuals (myself included) who seek to help nonprofits function better. And there are individuals who assist nonprofits in evaluating their services. But these resources are scarce, and there is seldom an adequate budget for them. Further, when they do occur, the individuals involved rarely get together with other individuals doing the same thing, so there is little "knowledge recapture." The big for-profit consulting firms, for example, milk the "float" of knowledge from each client to help all clients. The firms represent a storehouse of accumulated and processed knowledge about organizations, what makes them work well, what processes are useful, what kinds of things should be avoided, etc. Hence the consultations, theoretically at least, get better and better as the interventions are based on more and more knowledge. At the moment such organizations are just developing in the nonprofit field.

These are not the only problems that administration and management in social work agencies suffer but they will suffice. They are among the most important from a managerial perspective. The existence of such problems singly and severally, means that social work agencies, as a whole, are under led and under managed and over supervised. This situation occurs because managers and executives, shy of executive and managerial knowledge and experience revert to their default "supervisory" experience, which often means micromanagement, inbox clearing, and paper shuffling.

It means that we have problems with efficiency (doing things right) and effectiveness (doing the right thing). It means that we are not necessarily sure of what we are actually doing, or whether that action is doing any good. Do we, as someone once put it, make a difference? And if so, does that difference make any difference?

Remedies: Consultative help is not available or is episodic. We need to develop consultative capacity for the nonprofit field. One example might be the Forbes Fund, a supporting organization of the Pittsburgh Foundation (Pittsburgh, PA). Started in 1980 by my father, Elmer J. Tropman, it provided grants to help support consultants who work with nonprofits who needed help. Plans are afoot to develop in the Elmer J. Tropman Institute an organization to provide research and resources for nonprofits in Pittsburgh and the wider community. Other communities may also have such functions under development.

Other kinds of help are on the horizon as well. One of the commercial consulting firms mentioned previously, Bain & Co. of Chicago, is developing just such an entity. It is called the Bridge Group, and will offer services to nonprofits at rates they can afford. It will be staffed by Bain employees (who will work, at reduced pay, for specific periods of time at Bridge). (For a discussion of it see David Johnston, "Creating Waves in Nonprofit Sea," in the New York Times, February 2, 2000, p. c1;c12)

In both cases, the Tropman Institute and the Bridge Group, emphasis is both on specific helping and recapturing knowledge. Other organizations–the Fieldstone Alliance and the Conservation Company–provide assistance to nonprofits in the development of organizational capacity.

Wicked Problems

The structure and purpose of nonprofits, as I just explained, make their work difficult. However, the very nature of that work and the expectations surrounding it can be and are deeply problematic in their own right. Doing work in the human services is one of the most difficult organizations in which to be employed.

Reasons include the essential difficulty of their mission as well as a knotty complexity of the issues with which they have to deal. Furthermore, human problems seem to keep coming and coming and coming. There is no real end to the supply of them, or to the amount of work you might do with even a few. Rittel and Weber (1973), years ago developed a category of "wicked problems" which seems to describe the issues that human service managerial supervisors, project managers, and middle managers must deal with.[2] However, not all human services agencies deal with human problems directly. Funding and planning agencies, for example, deal indirectly with them. However, they become involved in the "wicked problem" discourse as they try to plan and fund; as they ask for data that does not exist; and as they seek evaluations that "are impossible." To some extent, those working indirectly with human problems may themselves share the "wicked problem" perspective, either because they came from a direct service agency or by their own temperament and disposition.

It is also true that all tasks that the direct service agency undertakes are not "human problem" tasks (projects like planning the annual meeting, or organizing a fundraiser). However, when relatively straightforward tasks exist in a "wicked problems" culture those tasks take on a "wicked problems" patina. To give one example, I was working with an agency which had an annual "thanksgiving basket" program, in which donated food was procured and thanksgiving meal baskets made up for families that could not afford such a meal. The Executive was complaining to me that this task seems to take more and more time every year. She asked me to look into it. I had to report back that the reason it took so long was that no protocols, notebooks, Gantt charts, etc. had ever been developed for this important piece of agency work. Each year whomever was assigned to "run" the program started from scratch and "asked around" for information from others who had (and had not!) done it before and what the "to do" list was. Naturally, the information was spotty, inaccurate, and arrived episodically. This practice usually resulted in a "thanksgiving crunch" in which all the agency staff were mobilized (along with the volunteers, who complained that they had not been notified until the last minute) to get the food, sort it, package it, decide who should get it, find out how big the families of the "who group" were so that an appropriate package could be put together and delivered it.

Everyone was so exhausted there was no time for agency celebration or recognition of the staff and volunteers who actually, finally, did it. The agency seemed to give no administrative thought to the project manager. The appointment process became "negatively charged." Because each year was "worse than the last" (in spite of promises each year to "fix this problem"), the employee who had just done it vowed never to do it again. Usually, there would be a new person (or someone with low power) who was then assigned to the job. I could go on, but you get the picture.

When I reported this situation to the Executive, and observed that most PTOs do better than this with their ice cream socials, she was troubled and aghast. "What do they do?" she asked. "Well," I replied, "they at minimum have a note book that lists all the things that need to be done and when, so that next year can run better than last year, not worse. They update the notebook every year with essential information, like telephone numbers, etc. And they have next year's person apprentice to this year's person." "But that would never work here" the Executive replied, "we are dealing with needy people whose needs always change; we have to be sensitive to that." "But," I pointed out, "needy or not, you provide the same product every year; you get lists from the same churches and agencies every year." "That is the problem with you people from the University" the Executive said, "you just do not know what it is like in the real world."

Needless to say my career at that agency was not an extended one. And it goes without saying that any Executive might well participate in wicked problems syndrome (WPS). So, as I will discuss in the section on people management, managers should begin with self examination and personal cleansing.

How Can Managers Lead in this Situation?

In terms of the WPS the most important things that a supervisor, project manager, and/ or middle manager can do, involve recognition of the dangers of WPS, and being alert to the issues and problems that it might present. In Figure 14 you will find ten "wicked problem" aspects and corresponding suggested managerial actions.

"Wicked Problems"

Wicked Problem Aspect	Suggested Managerial Actions
1. There is no definitive formulation of a wicked problem	Help your staff to develop a working definition of the problem currently "at the plate."
2. Wicked problems have no stopping rule	Set reasonable timelines for work.
3. Solutions to wicked problems are not false, but good or bad	Try to avoid the good or bad mindset; look for true or satisfactory options; recall that wicked problems cannot be "solved" anyway; they can only be "managed". Don't let the best be the enemy of the adequate.
4. There is no immediate and no ultimate end of a solution to a wicked problem	Given these problems, do not become embroiled test in "ultimate" discussions.
5. Every solution to a wicked problem is a "one-shot operation"; because there is no opportunity to learn by trial and error, attempt counts significantly	Try to develop lists of what works and what doesn't; work with employees to search for success pattern packages that can be taught to every others (harvesting).
6. Wicked problems have an innumerable (rather than and exhaustible describable) tential solutions; there is not a well-described set of permissible operations that may be incorporated into the plan	Considering 3 and 4 above, work to develop a few (three is good) options and pick one that set of po- seems most satisfactory.
7. Every wicked problem is essentially unique	Work to avoid this mindset. All problems do have unique elements; we as professionals are looking for the common ones.
8. Every wicked problem can be considered a symptom of another problem	Avoid becoming trapped in "the great chain of being." If you are working on substance abuse, stick to that, being mindful that "more" is "going on" but assist workers in achieving and sustaining focus.
9. The existence of a discrepancy representing a wicked problem can be explained in numerous ways. The choice of explanation determines the nature of the problem's resolution	Try to avoid being trapped in the ideology of cause, and look at the situation "on the ground". Develop a priority of interventions - triage in a way - and work with that.
10. The manager has no right to be wrong	We do make mistakes. Managers should actually encourage small ones; they tend to prevent the bigger ones.

Figure 14

A Cut Above

Finally, there is the pressure of social expectations. Adding to this set of pressures, however, there is the presence of higher expectations of the staff of non-profit organizations, relating to the service purpose of their mission. The higher purpose or civic purpose organizations nonprofit social service agencies, churches, philanthropies, etc., may create a stress of their own. These higher expectations are problematic in their own right. In addition, they may add even more problems because their stakeholders tend to think of nonprofits and their staff as "more pure" than corporate managers, and less vulnerable to the range of human venalities available. It is likely that nonprofit managers have this view of themselves.

Managers need to recognize that they (and all of us) are people and none of us are exempt from the problems and temptations that beset people everywhere and everyday. For personal peace of mind, the manager needs to recognize that he or she can do only so much. Managers also need to recognize that they have lives, family, and personal needs outside of work and that this is ok. Indeed, performance in all sectors will be better if you attend to needs in each sector and do not ignore any sector. Understanding oneself as fallible, permits greater understanding of others as fallible as well. Managerially, you must be alert for signs that problems might be developing. Indicators such as lying or omitting information, expense account padding, stealing office supplies, inappropriate use of the internet at work, etc. all these (perhaps small) problems are indicators of larger issues or steps on the journey to larger issues. Early and **DIRECT** confrontation is vital here. As the ad has it for parents and teenagers, urging parents to confront adolescents at the first sign of a substance issue, "**ACTION: THE ANTI DRUG.**"

Conclusion

Much needs to be done to improve the executive and governance cadres of social work agencies. Our road is long and arduous. We have a lot of baggage, baggage that we have been taught to carry. But in this, as in all things, we have choice. We can choose to hem and haw, to propose SOSO (same old same old), to claim lack of resources, lack of appreciation, lack of support and a bad back, or we can strive to be, as the ad for the American Army has it, "Be All That You Can Be." Our clients deserve no less.

---

[1]An earlier version of this chapter appeared as "Managerialism in Social Work" in the Hong Kong Journal of Social Work.

[2]Rittle and Weber developed the "wicked problems" concept to apply to public (i.e., governmental) managers. They fit well there, but also apply here. I discussed them in detail in Policy Management in the Human Services (Tropman, 1984, pp 32-33).

[3]The writing and training work of the Wilder Foundation has now become a separate organization: The Fieldstone Alliance. (fieldstonealliance.org)

Part 3

THE PEOPLE PICTURE:
Managing Five Ways

Introduction

Managers have two general foci for their work, people and products. They are of course interrelated, but there is enough difference to address them separately. The two emphases are listed in Figure 15. In the left-hand area are the people foci for managers – your managerial self, of course, subordinates, peers, bosses, and the manager's external network. Figure 15 illustrates these managerial targets in columns 1 and 2. Columns 3, 4, and 5 will be dealt with in Part 4 of this book (See page 79.)

The Supervisory / Managerial Grid

Supervisory / Managerial People Focus		Supervisory / Managerial Product Focus		
Management / Managing... Target		Tasks	Projects	Systems / Mission
Yourself / IN (within) (and family)		X	X	X
Your Subordinates (direct reports) / DOWN		X	X	X
Your Peers / ACROSS			X	X
Your Bosses / UP				X
Your External / OUT Network				X

Figure 15

Part 3 - Chapter 4

MANAGING ONESELF:
Avoiding the Department
of the Deeply Clueless

Introduction

When we think of management it is almost axiomatic that we look outward - somehow managing is managing "others." And indeed it is much that. However, that view circumvents the core of managerial centeredness, your own self. If you cannot manage yourself, then it is really not possible to manage much else.

Obviously this topic could be and has been the subject matter of volumes. Here, I draw on interviews with managers, as well as, the literature to highlight some of the most critical elements, and ones that are not infrequently overlooked. For discussion here we will touch upon stress and stress management, time management, issues of executive mental and physical health, temperament, emotional intelligence, and executive coaching. Part of managing yourself is managing your family (or managing with your family). Because this topic is so important I am including it here, as well.

Stress and Stress Reduction

The thing about stress is that not having any stress is not good. We all need some stress (recall the need for "challenge" mentioned earlier). The key issue involves preventing stress from becoming strain. Stress, in appropriate amounts, develops us; strain injures us. Obviously, then, the key is to prevent stress from becoming strain. A good start is to understand the different kinds of stressors that exist. The following list of the kinds of stressors is a start:

- Anticipatory: worry about what is to come
- Encounter: specific difficult people
- Time: never enough time
- Situational situations, like public speaking, that upset us.

With this list in mind (we can add detail ourselves) some of the techniques suggested below will certainly help.

Eliminate Stressors

Maintain physical and mental health. A healthy person has to have energy to deal with stress, no matter the kind. That is why we provide health tips a bit later in this chapter. As you lose energy, you run out of "cope." ("Cope" is my phrase for one's "ability to deal" on any given day. Fatigue can limit your supply of "cope," and success can increase your supply of cope.)

Develop Resiliency

Resiliency is a bounce back capacity that has physical as well as emotional components. It is part of what is called "optimism" in the emotional intelligence work (ability to "press on" in spite of setbacks). There is also a spiritual aspect, in the sense, to be mentioned in a moment, that "this too shall pass" and that you have a connection to a force larger than yourself. This sense of connection is vital, for example, in every Physical Health Assay program as on page 60.

Learn Temporary Coping Mechanisms

We all need some "quick copers" that help us manage stress on a daily basis. Some say a small prayer, others count to ten, listen to music, meditate, read a book, or whatever. Recharging and gathering your strength is of key importance and "quick copers" help you to avoid making situations worse, as well as to reenergize yourself.

One of the things about stress is that it robs us of our repertoire of interactional styles that we have available. Under stress, we tend to revert to our default style, whatever the one is that most defines us (see the section on temperament on page 61) and that we are most comfortable with, REGARDLESS OF HOW EFFECTIVE IT IS IN THE SITUATION. Stress tends to want to make us feel comfortable, and we begin to fly on "automatic." If you have ever moved, and "accidentally" driven, at the end of the workday, to you former home, you will know what I mean. That is why temporary coping mechanisms are especially important in areas of stress that are likely to force us to our default wall.

Time Management

One important stressor is time, or the lack of time. Time is a vital resource. It is the one thing we cannot get any more of. Time management issues generally fall into two big "pots," one is prioritization and two is schedule control.

Prioritization means understanding your ideal time distribution and the actual time distribution you have achieved or defaulted to or, well, whatever. The Index of Difference (see Figure 16) can help you understand your current situation. For illustration purposes I have made some assumptions. One is that there are five areas of life that are important (this is the "between sector application"). The five areas are listed in the left hand column. Though arbitrary, most of us would agree that these five areas are important, if not the only, sectors of value to us. I have also assumed an "ideal" distribution that my "ideal" individual selected. In Column 2, I assumed that his or her "real" distribution was as displayed, very heavily work oriented. There is almost no time for anything else. In Column 3, I show the absolute difference for each row (the absolute difference disregards sign). The final step is to add up the differences in Column 3 and divide by two. The resulting quotient, the Index of Difference, shows how far apart the "IDEAL" and the "REAL" distributions are. Now of course, it does not tell you if your ideal choices are "correct." You may want to go back and revisit them, and then recalculate. But if you have an Index of Difference of over 15% it probably means you are being sucked into one of the dimensions more than you wish. Typically, for managers, this happens with work. Work acts like a vacuum, dragging people into its vortex. First, civic time usually goes, and then personal time and finally some family time goes as well. Managers are often thrilled about the money they are making, not realizing they are working two jobs at the same workplace! Realization is the first step toward achieving mastery of schedule. Keep in mind that organizations are adept at getting people to work free or cheap; it is one of the ways they make money or break even. So if you choose to contribute, fine; if you do not, it is time for boundary setting and limit enforcement. It is good to remember that "work" can absorb all the time you have to give it and more; be sure that it is given voluntary.

Index of Difference

Life	Ideal	Real	Ideal – Real
Personal	25%	5%	20%
Family	25%	15%	10%
Work	25%	75%	50%
Civic	20%	5%	15%
Other/Misc.	5%	0%	5%
Total	100%	00%	100%/2 = an Index of Difference of 50%

Figure 16

Below is an empty example that you can use or copy for your own use. Give it a try! Ask your partner or spouse to fill out one as well and compare - they can do it for you, or you can do two sets - one each for ideals and one for real.

Life	Ideal	Real	Ideal – Real
Personal			
Family			
Work			
Civic			
Other/Misc.			
Total			Total/2 = Index of Difference

Strategic control requires schedule control. For successful managers, schedule control means TIME MANAGEMENT. Now that we know where we want to spend our time, we need to develop means through which to actualize, implement, or execute our strategy. For one thing, you can use the Index of Difference within sectors (say job, family, and/or personal) to sub-prioritize tasks within each of those and see if they are really important and how important.

Second, you need to use some kind of planning system - Franklin Planner™, Day Timer™, or whatever. Any system will do, as long as you use it. The Franklin Planner™ makes a special attempt to integrate strategic and tactical elements, with spaces to connect values to the day to day activity. Time management is very much like health management, fitness management, weight management, and so on. It needs to be integrated into your actual day to day work. It is a challenge, perhaps the first challenge a manager faces. Moreover, if you do not control your schedule, it will control you, and your Index of Difference will zoom out of sight.

Issues of Executive Mental and Physical Health

It may seem odd that managerial supervisors in social welfare should be reminded about mental health, and its importance. But then there is a bit of the shoemaker's child here, where you are most likely to ignore those things you are good at when it comes to yourself. As Abe Lincoln said, "A lawyer who defends himself has a fool for a client." At the Menninger Clinic (now moved to Houston, TX) they have a Professionals in Crisis (PIC) program. Based upon their work with professionals who have experienced and are managing crises, they have developed the following suggestions for positive mental health.

Tips from the Menninger Clinic (Abrams, 1990)

There are 19 points (see Figure 17) well worth keeping in mind that I have taken from Tips from the Menninger Clinic (Abrams, 1990) and "Mental Fitness Strategies" (Compass, November, pp.72-74). I have added some explanatory thumbnails to flesh out the concepts. Many on this list overlap others. They are not intended to be mutually exclusive, but rather a way to touch upon similar bases from a number of vantage points.

19 Points to Mental Health

Tip	Explanatory thumbnail from J. E. Tropman
1) Don't hide from yourself	Be as honest with yourself as possible about what is going on with you.
2) Be truthful about assets, liabilities, & needs	Be straightforward about your motives and your desires, as well as your deficiencies and areas where you need help.
3) Take time to reflect	Every day, spend a little time thinking and reflecting about the day and what happened and your reactions to it.
4) Know your feelings	Try to recognize and articulate to yourself, at least, what you are feeling and sensing. You may or may not share these with others as appropriate.
5) Know what can you take, job wise	Articulate to yourself what you can and cannot tolerate on the job, in terms of job conditions, treatment of yourself, etc. Revise these as appropriate in advance of precipitating events.
6) Don't narcotize	Avoid excessive alcohol and drug use as a way of handling the situation.
7) Make friends with change	Accept the fact that changes come whether you like it or not.
8) Learn to tolerate frustration	Find ways to tolerate the inevitable frustrations jobs bring without over involving your colleagues and family.
9) Watch out for your destructiveness-the darker side of your nature	Each of us has a destructive, revenge seeking side. Each of us also has the propensity to misuse power for personal reasons. Be alert to these (see also #1 & #4).
10) Be sure to set realistic goals	Goals that are too modest or too sever will not help you grow.
11) Don't compare yourself	Do benchmark – but against best practices and against your previous self. Comparisons tend to be self-denigrating.
12) Choose role models carefully	As you look around for models some people look really good; remember that what you see is not all you may get.
13) Prepare for possible loneliness	As you move up people in your workplace tend to move away; accept this.
14) Be philosophical	Remember that there is a larger world out there.
15) Attend to the spiritual side of life	We already mentioned the importance of spirituality earlier. Whatever that spirituality is for you, do not loose connection with it.
16) Pay attention to external forces	Look out as well as in and down. Change often comes from the outside.
17) Develop perspective	Very similar to #14, be able to take the immediate and the longer view.
18) Learn to trust others	Trusting others is vital; otherwise your time will be spent checking. Some will not deserve your trust, and you will have to take heat for their errors. Move on; do not trust more then once (this is not baseball; one strike is enough).
19) Keep growing	We can all learn all the time. The thing to keep in mind is that we need to learn from success and failures.

Figure 17

Maintain Physical Health

Maintaining your physical health is of vital Importance, but many of us overlook it. Physical health, as I mentioned a moment ago, is the physical source of energy, balance, and resiliency. Most people know they should take care of their physical health and when asked if they do, most reply "yes, I try."

But saying you try and take care of your physical health does not make it so. Listed in Figure 18 is a small physical health assay from "THE ONE MINUTE MANAGER GETS FIT" by Kenneth Blanchard, et al (1989). It is 12 questions that have been empirically shown to be highly important. Take it, and if your score is lower than you like, think of ways to improve your physical health. Most of us have work to do with weight control, cardiovascular fitness, strength building, getting better sleep, etc., but these are all goals we can set for ourselves as managers. It is part of managing yourself.

Physical Health Assay

(Disagree/No = 0;   Agree/Yes = 1)

1]   I love my job (most of the time)   _____

2]   I use safety precautions (ex: seat belts)   _____

3]   I am within 5 lb. of my ideal weight   _____

4]   I know 3 methods to reduce stress that do not involve
     drugs or alcohol   _____

5]   I do not smoke   _____

6]   I sleep 6 - 8 hr. each night and wake up refreshed   _____

7]   I engage in physical exertion at least 3 times a week -
     (sustained physical exertion of 20 -30 minutes -
     plus strength and flexibility)   _____

8]   I have 7 or fewer alcoholic drinks per week   _____

9]   I know my blood pressure   _____

10]   I follow sensible eating habits (eat breakfast each day,
      limit salt, sugar, fats, eat enough fiber, few snacks, etc.)   _____

11]   I have a good social support system   _____

12]   I maintain a positive mental attitude   _____

Total   _____

Score ...11-12 = an excellent Healthstyle ... 9-10 = a good Healthstyle ... 8 and lower = consider revisiting your Healthstyle

Figure 18

Temperament

We each have our styles and ways of doing things. There are many ways to assess your temperament. The Myers Briggs Type Indicator (MBTI) is perhaps among the best known, but there is also the Enneagram, and DiSC, which focuses on communication styles.[1] I do not recommend any one in particular. They all have strengths and weaknesses. What I do suggest is that you take time to find one temperament assay which you like, and familiarize yourself with it and think about it. The process of reflection and review is perhaps as valuable as any specific method. Keep in mind that, whatever you call it, each of us has a "default" style of interacting (recall from before in the discussion of stress). When someone asks the question "What is John Tropman like?" the answer will reflect my "default" style, for the most part. It is your core. Assays may not get at the entire core, but they do shed light on it, and that is important for each of us. Let me share a snapshot of the Myers Briggs perspective and its four key dimensions (MBTI).

According to Myers Briggs thinking, each of us has one dominant set of initials which defines our "type." However some of us are really strong with one or more dimensions (I myself have strong ratings on 3 of the 4; on the 4th, decision making, I am split, being both rule based and person based). It is the strong ones that require most attention, because they are the ones others notice most and the ones that tend to be "our personality" to others. I have listed some of the characteristics of each of the letters (see Figure 19 on page 62).

There are many sites on the web where you can take a MBTI. The only point here is to understand that our approach to daily life is structured, rather than random, has patterning and themes, rather than arbitrariness. They help others relate to us, but can also become rigid and repetitive.

Once you have a sense of your temperament, you can be more operationally aware of when its display is appropriate. Further, you can experiment with other temperaments/ styles. Myers Briggs analyses explicitly talk about the "Shadow Side," the temperament that is exactly the opposite from you. You are encouraged to explore that to broaden your repertoire.

There are two kinds of errors you can make in using temperament assays. One is to ignore them completely. If you take that path, then the ability to learn from the process of reflection is lost, and any specific information which might have some if not complete accuracy is also lost. The other error is to become too involved with any specific "self-portrait." Assays "reflect" you, rather than "define" you. Therefore "use it, don't refuse or abuse it."

Myers Briggs Snapshot

Dimension	Name/Letters	Thumbnail
SOURCE OF ENERGY - Where does your energy come from?	Extroversion vs. Introversion (E/I)	E = gets energy from others (Do -Think -Do) I = gets energy from being alone and reconstituting for a bit (Think- Do - Think)
GATHERING INFORMATION - Are you a forest or a tree thinker?	Sensing vs. Intuition (S/N)	S = fact based, 5 senses person (Step by Step) I = gut based, 6th sense person (Leaps about)
MAKING DECISIONS - Are you rule based or people based?	Thinking vs. Feeling (T/F)	T = rules based decision making (fair play and firm minded) F = feelings based decision making (fair share and tender hearted)
LIFESTYLE ORIENTATION - Do you prefer openness or closure?	Perceiving vs. Judging (P/J) (perceiving refers to preference for openness; judging refers to preference for closure.)	P = seeks openness (organized) J = let's wrap things up and move on (spontaneous)

Figure 19

Emotional Intelligence (The Emotion Quotient or EQ)[2]

I mentioned emotional intelligence (EQ) earlier when we were talking about feelings in the workplace. Failure to recognize and mange our own feelings is one of the important causes of managerial failure. Its stunning rise to wide application in managerial circles is proof that it has certainly uncovered an area of importance, even if you do not always agree with its specific points. I have outlined the following specific elements of EQ:

Specific Elements of EQ

- SELF AWARENESS
  - knowing what you feel
  - using instinct to make decisions you can live with (emotional intelligence)

- MANAGEMENT OF FEELING
  - controlling impulses
  - soothing your anxiety
  - having appropriate anger

- MOTIVATION
  - zeal, persistence and optimism in the face of setbacks emotional intelligence

- EMPATHY
  - reading and responding to unspoken feelings (someone crying in your office does not count!)

- SOCIAL SKILLS
  - handling emotional reactions in others
  - interacting smoothly
  - managing relationships effectively

These may seem obvious to those trained in the human services. However, as noted in the introduction to this chapter, we are really not any better than any other profession (and often times worse) when it comes to understanding ourselves. Therefore, as with temperament, it is a useful tool - but only a tool - to help us understand ourselves. One advantage to the EQ is that it has a range of tools you can use to assess yourself; in fact measuring EQ has become something of a cottage industry. The point is to use these assays, as with the MBTI, to get a perspective rather than a determination about you. I have included another such instrument (Figure 20) for your consideration. Of course you can "cheat" on it and make yourself look good; but it is a little like "sneaking drinks"; each tells you there is an issue you need to confront. Once again, the assessment is a picture, not a bronze, of you. If you did score lower, then you might want to consider some steps to increase your EQ.

The EQ Assessment
(taken from USA Weekend September 8-10, 1995)

Questions 1, 2, 5, 7, 8, 9, 11, & 12 use reverse scoring:
- always = 0
- usually = 1
- sometimes = 2
- rarely = 3
- never = 4

Questions 3, 4, 6, & 10 use positive scoring:
- always = 4
- usually = 3
- sometimes = 2
- rarely = 1
- never = 0

1. I am aware of even subtle feelings as I have them   _____

2. I find myself using my feelings to help make big decisions   _____

3. When I am angry I blow my top or fume in silence   _____

4. Bad moods overwhelm me   _____

5. I can delay gratification in pursuit of my goals
   instead of getting carried away by impulse   _____

6. When I am anxious about a challenge I can't prepare well   _____

7. Instead of giving up in the face of setbacks, I stay hopeful   _____

8. People don't have to tell me what they feel – I can sense it   _____

9. My keen sense of other's feelings gives me compassion
   about their plight   _____

10. I have trouble handling conflict and emotional upset   _____

11. I can sense the pulse of a group and unspoken feelings   _____

12. I can soothe my distressing feelings so they don't keep
    me from doing what I have to do   _____

Total   _____

Scores.... 36+ means your EQ is Excellent….. 25-36 means your EQ is Good/ Usual…. Below 25 you could use some work on your EQ

Figure 20

Executive Coaching

Managing yourself is difficult to begin with, and even more difficult to do alone. You need help. My recommendation is that every manager secures an executive coach. A coach is not a mentor, though they may perform some mentor-like functions. A coach is someone you actually pay to help you. A mentor is usually a friend or colleague who is willing and happy to help ... up to a point. The problem is you do not really know where that point is. Managers can borrow a page from a therapist's notebook here. All competent therapists have a didactic therapist who reviews cases with them and raises issues that their "pupil" might wish to consider.

It is important to find someone to whom you can talk on a regular basis and who knows both managerial issues and your sector. The costs should be somewhere between $100 and $200/hour. Now you might be thinking "Whoa ... Who has THAT kind of money ... not me!" You do have that kind of money. It is in investment in your future. Your coach is one of the array of professionals you have available to help you with your life (lawyer, plumber, etc.) Invest in yourself. The coach will be able to guide you to readings and websites of importance, key conferences, and will typically do some kind of initial assay to get a feel for who you "are" and what your "default" style is. Naturally, you get supervision at your workplace. In nonprofits especially, though, as I mentioned in Chapter 3, programs for and support of managerial development are extremely thin. Indeed, as I also mentioned, appreciation for the managerial enterprise is often lacking in whole or in part. You can rail against the unfairness of this, or simply say "If I wait for my agency to help me, I will be long gone." Budget some resources for your own development. It has a great rate of return. Further, there are some things that you really do not want to raise at your agency, such as your plans to look for a better job. It is good to have someone to talk those ideas and procedures over with. That is the purpose of a coach. You do not have to use a coach on any regular basis, by the way. After an initial assessment purpose, the coach should be manager-activated. Sometime you will need to talk with that person a couple times a week for a while, then not for many months. It really depends on what is going on with you and your work. Usually a yearly managerial check up is a good idea, but beyond that, it is up to you.

In addition to the coach, you might want to get together with a group of executives from your area that are about your same age/position, etc. You can call it a "reading group," if you like. It can be all women (especially important for women because women have less support in managerial roles than men), all men, mixed, whatever. It is good to have a "pretext" to use in getting together, because setting up a group, especially among males, which implies that we are in less than complete control and want to discuss our "issues" seems, regrettable, to often lack support. Hence the indirect method works better than the direct one.

Managing Your Family

This topic is, again, one that could stand volumes of attention. And it is heavily gendered in many of its issues. Looking overall, family management is a combination of all the kinds of management - self, peer, subordinate, boss, and external. It is a complex of managerial demands and activities. For one thing there is work-life balance, something I discussed before in the section on the Index of Difference. Remember that we work for ourselves, but also for our families. If success at work means that your family never sees you, this is perhaps, problematic. Balance between work and family is key. There is an old story James Thurber wrote about the drinking bear that illustrates this point. He would drink, and crash around breaking furniture and making a mess. He went into ABA (Alcoholic Bears Anonymous), got a personal trainer, became extremely fit, and would illustrate this by crashing around, breaking furniture, and making a mess. The moral is that "You may as well fall flat on your face as lean too far over backward!" - (Thurber, 1945, p.253)

Family management is a cooperative enterprise, for the most part, and one in which your partner or spouse needs to be involved. We should all remember the "success/ sacrifice" equation. Everyone's success depends to some extent on the sacrifices of others, whether we recognize it or not. We need to surface and examine the sacrifices, and see if upon that examination, everyone feels they are worthwhile.

In today's family, spouses and partners of managers are likely to be professional as well. This means that there are frequently two careers to manage, not one. Issues of sequencing, primacy, timing, and many others need to be discussed, preferably in advance. Of course, the complexity of these issues makes for an increased level of sensitivity and difficulty for these conversations. But another problem is that managers often forget to use their managerial skills in the family setting. It is for this reason, I included a chapter on the "family meeting" in my new edition of Meetings: How to Make Them Work for You (2nd) (2002). Many of these family career meshing issues need to be discussed in, well, meetings. But having a "family meeting" seems so odd and weird, even though that is exactly what managers would do at the office (I am not saying they go well there, either, which was the reason for the book in the first place.) If possible, work at actually having a family meeting with you and your spouse or partner (and older children too) to consider the range of family interests and ways in which those interests might be addressed and the optimal solutions generated. It may sound even funnier, but a longer range family plan is a good idea as well. I know several families who have "strategic plans" of a sort. They are thinking ahead, but flexible too, as situations evolve and change.

Women managers have special issues and problems. If there are children in the family, they usually have, as Hochschild says in "The Second Shift" (1989; 2003), a totally second job before they leave and when they get home from work. For many women, work is a relaxation, a place filled with respect, deference, appreciation, and little pee and pooh. Women managers often feel guilty when at work and when not at work. They especially need the support and affirmation from other working moms.

Families have a complex set of needs and requirements. As an organization (to take that narrow view for a moment) they are a challenge. When you add in the emotions that bind and separate families, as well as complicated and often unacknowledged role expectations (of self, partner, and children relatives) it is astonishing that they are as successful as they are. The periodic public mantras about "family values" are, to me, a sort of sad reflection that many people have no idea as to how to manage modern family life. They are totally (or mostly) flummoxed, and resort to platitudinous vocalizations as a substitute for practical managerial family work. Problematic workplace events only add stress to a family larder that is already full. That said the appropriate application of a few managerial principals can make a big difference. But like other applications, this is not an "off the shelf" kind of thing, but a customized one, tailored to each family's specific needs, wants, habits, and patterns.

Conclusion

The topics mentioned in this chapter - stress and stress management, time management, issues of executive mental and physical health, temperament, emotional intelligence, and executive coaching - are all huge and popular. Thousands of sites for each can be found on the internet, a testimony to their centrality in our lives, and not only our managerial lives. The "family management" topic is a little different. There, the pattern is not so clear. While there are lots of internet entries such as the search engine Google, they are mainly focused on family businesses and family finances (and several on managing a family chicken flock). Hence source materials are a bit harder to come by in that area. That only tells us what we already knew - family management is a developing area, and one that needs careful thought and attention.

In spite of the plethora of materials in most areas, however, those who work with managers generally feel they lag in self awareness and self development. Many managers find themselves motoring along until they hit some organizational wall, and then turn around and ask "Whaaaaat?" As we will see in a later chapter on derailment, losing your job, being passed over, or being reassigned to "Siberia" comes as a shock to the "victim" but usually is no surprise to others in the workplace or family.

As a manager-to-be, a fledgling manager, or a full-fledged manager it is important not to wait until stuff hits the fan. Then it is too late. Move the stuff or adjust the fan proactively. The first place to start is with you.

[1]The web has many MBTI has many essays you can use, and others (D.S.C.)
[2]The web also has indicators for the EQ

Part 3 - Chapter 5

MANAGING SUBORDINATES:
Building Staff Performance

Introduction

In building staff performance, whatever the skill package, you should start with goals. These are the things to strive TOWARD. While the content of goals will always depend upon the situation, their architecture is always rather similar. Consider the following devices as structural suggestions to help succeed at goal setting.

There are two types of goals (SMART and SUCCESS) that you can consider. SMART goals are Specific, Manageable, Achievable, Realistic, and Time bound. SUCCESS goals are Simple, Understandable, Competence driven, Communicated clearly, Equitable, Sustain enthusiasm, and Share vision. If they do not meet those criteria, then you might want to redo your goals so they do.

Structuring the Managerial Architecture

Managerial supervisors need a system to follow through with workers. The first step is, as just mentioned, goal setting and the second step is monitoring. The frequency of monitoring varies, as some workers need more and others less. But you work toward only occasional checking. The third step is milestones. Usually this involves agreed upon milestones. A milestone is a significant output, necessary to achieving an outcome. Assessment is usually done in thirds or quarters, over however long the time period for the project. If there is a 90 day project, then every month might work. This occurs so that there can be "mid course corrections," if any needed. Finally, at the end of the project there is an appraisal. This is followed by what the military calls the "after action report" which deals with what happened in each case. From the after action report, or really at the conclusion of that report, there is a "lessons learned" section. These lessons become part of the harvesting process through which organizational learning occurs.

Goal Setting

Performance appraisal looks over the total performance of the worker for a year, or any defined period of time. This process is distinct from, but related to, the project assessment discussed above. The project appraisals become a part of the overall performance appraisal. It is important to give periodic and frequent feedback as to project performance. This process is called the performance audit. In the case of child welfare workers, the audit might focus on batches of cases.

As we look over the range of worker performance, it is important to look at the overall distribution of types of workers as every site will vary. However, there are some general guidelines which might be helpful. The first of these is the staff version of the modified 80:20 rule. A common statement of that rule is that 80% of your results come from 20% of your workers. That seems a bit on the extreme side, but a more reasonable version is as follows:

> - 20% of your workers are excellent
> - 60% are satisfactory
> - 20% are unsatisfactory or subpar

There is a lot of agreement among working managers that these proportions are generally accurate, though as I said, individual workplaces do differ.

The managerial problems of this average, though, are standard as well. Lots of time is given to those at the bottom; minimal time is given to the middle (with more being allocated as workers get closer to the bottom) and very little to the top 20%. As you can see, the presence of problematic workers is a double cost to you; nonproductive workers drain your time and keep you from assisting the regularly productive and super productive workers. Generally, your time should be proportional to the worker types - 20/60/20. If you spend much more than 20% of your time with the unsatisfactory or sub par workers, that is a problem.

We can actually break this down a bit more through looking at worker behavior as made up of success and failures. Consider the success/failure grid illustrated on the next in Figure 21. It is important to consider a worker's position on the success failure grid, as illustrated. Managerial supervisors should locate their particular staff within this grid and base their time appropriately. Keep in mind that the most problematic, really, are the shooting star workers. They are problematic because they are GOOD AND BAD. In that combo managerial supervisors are often likely to overlook the bad until it becomes really bad. The workers themselves are often likely to overlook their own problems as well, focusing on the good things they also do. This can make for a deadly combination.

The Success / Failure Grid

		Things Gone Right		
		Few	Some	Many
Things Gone Wrong	Few	1. So So Worker 10%	2. Satisfactory 10%	3. Excellent Worker 20%
	Some	4. Problem Worker 10%	5. Satisfactory 10%	6. Good Worker 20%
	Many	7. Problem Worker 10%	8. So So Worker 5%	9. Shooting Star Worker 10%

Figure 21

In the grid, managers should employ "differential use of self" not only in terns of time, but direction of work with these individuals. More on this point will be shared in the next chapter. For now, suffice it to say that for workers in Cells 4 and 7 (problem workers), managers should move toward outplacement. They are not doing much right and they are doing many things wrong. It is time to move on. Workers in Cells 1 and 8 (so so workers) need specific, tight, corrective action plans. If correction does not follow, we again move toward outplacement. Cells 2, 5, and 6 (satisfactory and good workers) need support and development.

Some managers, with whom I talked, especially those in human services, felt that having "outplacement" agendas for 35% of your workers was draconian (Cells 1, +4 +7 +8). Of course, that would be true if you used some kind of forced ranking system. But if you do an honest appraisal of your work teams, you should not be tolerating people in those cells for very long. Not only do they not do the job (Problem 1), and steal your time (Problem 2), but they also poison the workplace through bad examples and undermine the work you are doing with others (Problem 3) and finally, they make you look bad because you are NOT taking action (Problem 4). Moreover, outplacement is not the initial option. There is a sense of proportionality about it as you do try to be helpful. But remember, the reason you are in business is not to help the worker; it is to help the client/customer/consumer. You are paying the worker to assist the agency in that function. As the old saying has it, "if they are not part of the solution, they are part of the problem."

I saved Cells 3 (excellent workers) and 9 (shooting star workers) for last because they, rather than the "outplacement cells," represent the most serious problems you face. It is here that your energy should be centrally placed, and the two groups represent two entirely different patterns of concern. Oddly, the excellent workers in Cell 3 seem hardly a problem at all. The difficulty is that we are most inclined to ignore them. After all things are going well, exceptional even, and we have no real reason to interfere. Some managers even rationalize NOT attending to them on the grounds that "If it ain't broke, don't fix it" and "Leave well enough alone," etc. The point is though, that these workers need support and appreciation just as we all do. Their excellence no doubt involves them going the extra mile, and a bit of recognition is important for all humans. And remember, they have the most options. Excellent workers always have options, as other agencies which would love to get their hands on them. Not treating them well significantly increases your risk of losing them. They can, and will, leave.

Cell 9 (shooting star workers) is a completely different issue or at least mostly different as I mentioned a moment ago. Here we have workers who are doing an outstanding job, like those in Cell 3, but also screwing up badly as well. In many ways these are the most difficult to deal with because it is hard to discuss problems in the face of achievement. And because they are good and bad, they use their good (even from themselves) to blunt their bad. They tend, as do we all, to lionize our achievements and minimize the failures. Because their problems are the most likely to go unattended, undiscussed, and/or unremedied, they have the potential, and often realize this potential, to grow very large. These problems then grow to involving not only the shooting star worker, but also the entire agency and agency community (Tropman and Sheafer, 2004). Managers need to emotionally and empirically prepare themselves for meeting with these individuals and doing it sooner rather than later. Also, while full acknowledgment of the positives needs to be made, it must be made clear that this meeting focuses upon the problem areas. A good way to do this is to email the individuals in question with a complimentary introduction, and a list of the problematic areas, and a question for the respondent about how they intend to address these issues. Then the manager asks for a note before the meeting, so that the manager has a chance to review it. Tight structure is vital here.

Conclusion

Managers need to be careful of the allocation of their effort, for their own mental health if for no other reason. The other reasons are important though, and they essentially have to do with supporting and encouraging those who are doing well, appropriately attending to those who are not, and encouraging those in the middle. Special attention needs to be paid to those who are doing exceptionally well, but also have some exceptional screw-ups. One tendency is to ignore the excellent workers, leaving them feeling unappreciated. They need special attention as well. After all, they are the ones who produce much of your value.

Part 3 - Chapter 6

MANAGING FROM THE SECOND POSITION:
Managing, Bosses, Peers and Your External Network: Working Up, Across and Out

Introduction

Managing "in" (yourself and your family) and "down" (subordinates) are two of the "managing five ways" focus of this part for the book. The remaining three involve managing across (peers), "up" (your boss), and "out" (elements of your external network, which may include external peers). Recall our definition of management - accomplishing work through others. Sometimes those others involve peers, bosses, and external individuals. But in conventional understandings of management you have responsibility with no authority. That is what "managing from the second position" means.

I suppose we could divide the five ways of managing into two types - management with authority and management without authority. Each area has its problems, of course. When there is authority present, managers feel uptight and anxious when managing subordinates because they feel completely responsible for everything the subordinate does. This feeling creates a tendency to use the "Because I said so" approach or the "My way or the highway" option as the core technique, or at least one of the core techniques.

On the other hand, in the peer, superior, and external management venues, the opportunity to order anyone to do anything is virtually nonexistent. Hence, you have to build relationships, connect to the target, and get the target to "want to do" what it should do anyway. Unfortunately, many managers continue to use their "subordinate" approaches when they proceed into the "voluntary" arena of peers and external relations. They may also invert themselves when they are interacting with their bosses, hence be essentially a "lion" to subordinates and a "lamb" with their bosses. None of these techniques works very well over time. Unfortunately, the issue of legacy and organizational value are not being successfully addressed. Managers need to measure themselves not only by whether they got the job but by legacy as well.[1] And of course there is the issue of whether the organization and its legacy is a success to consider.

Managing Your Boss

The boss is perceived as the most crucial individual in your network because generally the boss is the one person who can fire you. If the boss does not fire you, he or she can make your life either miserable or great. Thus, establishing good relationships with the boss becomes crucial. The way to approach this is to think of your boss as someone to be "managed," not in a sly way, or a way that "spins" information to get what you want, but one which treats the boss as a customer (an internal customer).

Rule #1 Managing your boss well is to manage yourself well. Remember, the boss basically wants you to help the boss, not the reverse. If your actions create traffic into the boss's office, or problems for the boss to solve, you have failed to implement Rule #1.

Rule #2 Start where the boss is, style wise. Generally, you do this by understanding, first, the bosses preferred styles. As Steven Covey says, "seek first to understand, then to be understood" (1990). Our bosses, like us, have temperaments. They have preferred ways to get energy, to get information, to make decisions, and for openness or closure. Some work "on the fly," others like regular meetings of a more formal sort. Some like talking first, and reading second; others like to read a proposal first, and then talk about it. Your first approach is to give the boss information in the way the boss wants it.

Rule #3 Show commitment to the organization. Successful organizations reflect first on the boss. Representing the agency may involve doing a little extra work and then representing the organization and acting on behalf of it. Just be careful you do not always get in that role.

Rule #4 Focus your efforts for impact. Select the issues you bring to the boss very carefully.

Rule #5 Exhibit courage and honesty, with tact. We all do stupid things, bosses included. If you need to point out a problem, or disagree with the boss, do it diplomatically and privately, never in public. If you are "trapped" in a meeting where a boss says, "Everyone agrees, right?" You can say, "It certainly sounds good; let me just run over a few details and I will get back to you later today." The more the boss wants something, the less likely employees are to disagree, especially in public.

Rule #6 Involves working with the boss. Get the boss in the loop early, and make a work plan with the boss. Get both positive and negative feedback on the plan and on your progress. It is good to use the Index of Difference to rate the differences in emphases you and the boss may have with respect to projects. Often this is a real source of friction.

Rule #7 Get the boss in the loop early on issues that the boss might have special interest or which might be politically sensitive. Bosses, like all of us, hate to be surprised.

Rule #8 Help the boss look good. Bosses, like the rest of us, like to look good and need to look good. This means giving the boss positive feedback and occasionally, (though perhaps not as much as they "deserve"), also negative feedback. Portions of this rule involve not upstaging the boss. Remember, looking good in front of the boss is good as long as your looking good does not make your boss look bad.

Rule #9 Review the material for managing yourself, managing peers and external individuals and apply as appropriate!

Rule #10 Do Not forget rules 1-9!

Obviously these rules are not the end of the boss-managing road. But they will help you think about a thoughtful, planful, and proactive interaction with the boss that will minimize trouble for you.

Managing Your Peers

Managing peers involves getting cooperation, follow through, and execution (from those more or less equal to you) in the organization, but over whom you have no direct authority. It refers, as well, to the other employees of the organization. Thus, cooperation is, in a sense, voluntary. And they, of course, need you as well. All the issues that have been discussed in terms of managing your boss are important here and can be applied to managing your peers. And of course there is the material as well from managing yourself.

The peers I am talking about here are internal to your organization. And there are really two groups of peers. First, those who have similar or identical positions to you. This means other workers, other planners, and/or fellow professionals. They are peers whether or not they are at the exact same organizational level or not. Then there is everyone else in the organization (the support staff, the parking lot guy, and the copy machine person, etc.). In all cases, you need to pay attention to the quality of a relationship.

First, peer management is a relationship game. You are managing through building up positive connectivity so that, when you need their help, they will be happy to assist you in your project. This means that you must treat them with respect and express appreciation for their contribution to the organization, even if (perhaps especially if) your compliment does not refer to the work they did on your behalf. For that, a thank you is expected.

Second, you need to connect with them on some kind of regular basis - for coffee, lunch, a chat. This is especially true with professional peers. Find out how they are doing, and if they could use any help from you. An offer of help is worth a lot, even if they do not need it.

These interactions also allow you to update them on what you are doing and how it might impact them. Most organizations barely have adequate systems of organizational intelligence, and, therefore, much of the information passes through the informal system. Letting a coworker know that your project might have some impact on what they are doing keeps them in the loop. They in turn are likely to let you know when what they are doing might affect you.

There are some types of peer relations as well, you need to avoid. The difficult types of peers involve variations of the social credit/social debit rules of organizations. Years ago, in a book called Small Town in Mass Society, the authors Vidich and Bensman explored the age-old truth that small towns were friendlier and it was easy to go next door and borrow the proverbial "cup of sugar" (1958; 2000). They found it was true, you could easily borrow a cup of sugar. But, it was also true that they remembered you borrowed a cup of sugar. Organizations are a lot like small towns. There is social debit and social credit - people notice how much you draw out, and how much you put in.

You do not even have to pay back the sugar to the same person who you borrowed it from, but do pay it back to someone. So the saying "neither a borrower nor a lender be" is really wrong. We all need help, and need to give help. Good peer management involves investment in peers, formally and informally. Not all investments pay off, but then they are not all intended to pay off.

One peer relationship you should avoid is the "HiHowAreYa" colleague. All organizations have them. The HHAY is one who never calls except when she or he wants something. When that phone rings, they could not be friendlier, closer, or warmer. You KNOW they want something from you. But when you need their help they are always "slip-sliding away."

A second is the "what is in it for me" person. They will help but they want pay back right away. Watch out, too, for the person who wants to give help but on their own terms, not the terms in which you need. Some help is really a hindrance. The most hindering kind of help is the kind that actually sets you back. For this person it is like you were getting help from a combination of Inspector Clouseau and Mr. Magoo.

As time goes on we all have reputations as colleagues. We are continually rated in some invisible sociological amalgam that takes in all our contributions, positive and negative, and spits out a "rep." "Reps" can change but make no mistake, we all have them. And we all employ them as well. Each of us has our own list of "trustys," "dependables," or whatever you want to call them, who we help and on whom we call for help.

And of course peers in the organization, as I mentioned, can be of a professional nature, but it is important to never forget that the agency is made of human peers as well. These human peers include support staff, cleaning staff, etc. Good manners are always appropriate. Pleasant greetings, informal chats make you among those for whom support staff will go the extra mile. For the rest, they are referred to the sign that shows a character doubled over with laughter, the caption reads "YOU WANT IT WHEN??????"

Managing Your External Network

The same principles that apply to peers apply to the external environment. Building a network is important outside, as well as inside the organization.

It is good to have folks outside the organization with whom you talk and connect with on a regular basis. This is useful because everyone in the agency shares, along some dimension, the culture of the agency itself. It is useful to have some people who are outside the culture of the agency, and even outside the culture of your particular line of business, since industries and professions tend to share certain assumptions across agencies. I call this your community cabinet. It might include friends, your priest, minister, or rabbi, people in whom you have confidence. It should include your partner or spouse, but be careful, as partners and spouses have "axes to grind" as well.

One thing that is somewhat different though, between the internal and external groups (managing across and managing out), is the relationship between managing issues and managing people. Managing across tends to start with people (the relationship) and then brings issues together around those people. Managing out tends to start with issues and brings people together around them. That means there are some issue management considerations to keep in mind when managing out. And it is important to say that these same considerations can be applied in other management efforts.

One issue management technique is bundling. Bundling refers to the actual package of issue elements you include or do not include in your issue package. You are thinking here about what kind of people might sign on or turn off depending upon what piece is in (or is not in) the issue package that you present.

A second technique is framing, which refers to the way in which you make the case for their involvement (or for them to "stay out of this one"). It means articulating both the business and cultural reasons which should guide their decisions. These need to be thought out in advance because it is hard to be creative on the spot.

A third technique is involvement. At what point in the issue development process do you involve other stakeholders, and which stakeholders, and how intensively? One thing to keep in mind is the concept of "buy in." We have all heard managers say that they need to get "buy in" from the community, from other professionals, whatever. However, all too often the issue is bundled and framed and THEN buy in is sought. It is good to keep in mind that, after all, this is the country of the Boston Tea Party and the idea of "No Taxation without Representation." Buy in requires build in; if stakeholders are involved at the front end, the back end is much more pleasant.

Conclusion

Generally, each of these techniques can be considered "leading from the second position" (Kanter, 1977). As I noted in the chapter introduction, these techniques lead to situations in which "power" is ambiguous. In many ways this ambiguity is a good thing, because successful management relies on influence more than power. The use of power is a possible option and somewhat useful where resistance is high and there is not a lot of time for "process" options. "What of authority?" you might ask. Authority is just power where resistance is illegitimate, as with "resisting arrest." The chapter title - Managing from the Second Position is really backwards. Power and authority is the second position, and managing volunteers of one sort or another is really the most common, and hence, first position.

The problem with contemporary discourse is that it tends to assume that power/ authority is the sine qua non or the essential element of the management, when in fact it is a hugely complicating factor. Why? For one thing, authority is a sometime thing, dependent in large part on the subordinate recognizing and accepting that authority. This is a truth that every parent of an adolescent knows.

Secondly, in order to make authority work you need to use threats and inflict, or threaten to inflict, pain. While threats work up to a point, they will not work if people are unmoved (Gandhi, for example or other nonviolent movements) and they are costly. The more pain needed, the more the resistance; the more the resistance then the more resources are called into enforce the order; the more the forces, the more the cost, both in terms of direct application but also in terms of thinner coverage elsewhere.[2] Hence, even where authority is present, master managers find that pretending it does not exist and seeking cooperation and commitment is a wise course. Managing from the "second" position, then, is the first job of every manager. If you can perform martial arts with a blindfold, then seeing with no blindfold makes everything a piece of cake.

---

[1]See Chapter 16 on executive calamity and Chapter 17 on managerial success.
[2]In the 2004 Presidential campaign, Mr. Bush and Mr. Kerry wound up in the same small Iowa town on the same morning, just a few blocks from each other. Security was tight. That day the town had three bank robberies.

Part 4

THE PRODUCT PICTURE: Getting Jobs Done, Tasks and Work Accomplished

Introduction

The previous section looked at the people part of management. In that perspective, jobs tasks and work tended to "float"; we were not focusing on the product. In this section the emphases are reversed. It is now the job, the tasks, and the work that become the center of attention and the people "float". It may be helpful for you to refer to Figure 15 (below), which I used in the introduction to Part 3. It might help as well to recall Figure 1 (repeated on p. 80), with which I began. Our focus here is on columns 2, 3, and 4 in Figure 1.

The Supervisory / Managerial Grid (Repeated from page 53)

Supervisory/Managerial People Focus		Supervisory/Managerial Product Focus		
Management / Managing... 0Target		Tasks	Projects	Systems/Mission
Yourself / IN (within) (and family)		X	X	X
Your / DOWN Subordinates (direct reports)		X	X	X
Your Peers / ACROSS			X	X
Your Bosses / UP				X
Your External / OUT Network				X

Figure 15

Position, Responsibility, Focus and Activities on the Managerial Staircase (Repeated from page 2)

Position	Responsibility	Focus	Activities
1. Supervisory Manager	Jobs	Assignments	Oversight
2. Project Manager	Tasks	Projects	Organize
3. Middle Manager	Work	Systems/Mission	Orchestrate

Figure 1

Part 4 - Chapter 7

MANAGING JOBS

Introduction

The beginning of management is supervisory management. Most managers think that supervision begins when they are given a person to "boss." Who is the first person you need to "boss?" It really begins when you are given a job. That is why self-supervision is so important. You yourself are your first direct report. But whether you have yourself, alone, or several other direct reports, you essentially have three foci: the job, the assignments within the job, and overseeing completion of the assignments.

Assignments: The Essential Job

The job is your job description, or the job description of the direct report. We all know that those job descriptions are wish lists that almost no one could complete. And to make matters even worse, they often end with the laconic "other duties to be assigned," which means that the job description has virtually no meaning. That, however, is not entirely true. It is perhaps better called a "job scaffolding," under which your job is constructed. Your first task in supervisory management is to extract an "essential job" out of the myriad of things that are either on the job description list or that could possibly be done. This is true whether the supervisee is yourself, or a direct report. What this extraction means is that you select out of all the jobs, the package to which you must attend (if managing yourself) or the package that you want your direct report to attend. Usually, this process is one of negotiation, in which you, the supervisor, have certain priorities (must do's) and some other things that you would like to see done. Usually, the employee has some interests as well, and some of these, but not all, may match-up with your own. But it is usually possible to reach a compromise on an assignment package.

The list or package of assignments is one thing to complete, which is difficult enough. What is also necessary is to articulate the **weights** or time emphasis that you expect: a) to be allocated to the work and/or, b) that you expect the work to be done within. This is called the "effort ratio." It means how much of all your time should be spent on this aspect of the essential job. Failure to articulate these weights leads to a huge source of misunderstanding downstream. You can use the Index of Difference discussed earlier to assess the weights and their differences (if any) between you and your supervisee.

Oversight: The Means/Ends Chain

The second task you have is to make sure that the assignment completion is of quality. This requirement is placed on both process and outcome. Quality means and quality ends are essential. This dual focus is always important, but quality thinkers approach the reasons for these two qualities differently. Some think that a quality process always produces a quality outcome; therefore unsatisfactory outcomes are the result of problems in previous processes. There is truth in this assertion, but it misses two essential components. One is that exogenous factors may influence outcomes, factors that the process did not consider. True, but then no process can do everything. However, some might say, the failure to anticipate those variables is a failure of process. Well, ok, but 'stuff happens" whether you plan for it or not. This "stuff" may include things like effacement in budgetary allocation with no parallel change in responsibility, governmental changes, to say nothing of global events such as terrorism that can thrown any schedule into disarray.

The second problems are endogenous factors. In this problem set, it is not things from the outside that "crop up" to interfere with outcomes; it is a failure to anticipate all the internal elements that could create roadblocks for success. For example, managers might rely on a certain motivation level of staff, one similar to their own, only to find that staff are really not as motivated for project success as the manager is.

What these considerations mean is that the supervisor, project manager and middle manager must inspect process and outcomes, means and ends. To ignore process (results only based on management) invites manipulation of the process to produce the desired results, often at questionable quality. To ignore outcomes on the assumption that proper means will produce proper ends ignores external changes and internal ones, which can make an excellent product or outcome irrelevant. This is sometimes called "fighting the last war."

Basically, outcomes are nested in a means ends chain, and managers must dip into that chain at various points to be sure that means and ends are functioning and synchronous. If "a chain is only as strong as its weakest link" then, this old saying applies to the means ends chain as well. Hence, managers must find out where the most vulnerable and critical areas of the chain are, and pay special attention to those points. In performing these checks, the manager must seek a middle group.

The 30,000 foot manager (the high flyer) is one who has no feel for what is going on "on the ground." The micro manager (ground sniffer) is one who is too involved to see the larger picture. In both cases managerial actions act as a demotivator, tending to produce and reproduce exactly the behavior they are seeking to discourage. High flyers and ground sniffers both produce low quality.

Quality: Unacceptable, Acceptable, Better, Best and Exceptional

Over time, the routine and the regular operation of the means ends chain will produce outcomes of acceptable quality. But defining acceptable quality is very hard to define clearly, especially in human service work. This difficulty leads to the third task - defining acceptable performance in terms that you and the supervisee agree on. Defining "acceptable" means, obviously, defining "unacceptable." Of course you should not stop at "acceptable." Being "acceptable" is "good." That leaves "better," "best," and "exceptional." Managerial supervisors need to define those levels as well. Also, the consequences of being "unacceptable" need to be spelled out. "Good" is that below which the organization cannot fall without people losing their jobs. "Better" and "best" are the goals to strive for. "Exceptional" is always out there, waiting to be achieved. If you were to put these levels into a standard grading form, then D would be "unacceptable," C - "acceptable," B - "better/best," and A would be "exceptional."

Thinking along the lines of customer service, a D might be defined as "take it or leave it." This is what we offer and if you do not like it that is just too doggone bad. C might then be defined as "here is our service and if you complain and make a fuss we will adjust, but you must push us to do so." In the B range ("better and best"), we have substantial improvements, involved with anticipating the customer. "Better" (B-) means that we anticipate what you the customer might need and try to provide it. B+ means that we really do provide it. An A ("exceptional") refers to surprise and delight. The customer is not only "anticipated" but is also "blown away."

Moreover, "customer" is not just the external customer, the "client" "consumer," or whatever we call the service user. There are internal customers as well. Your spouse or partner is your "customer"; your kids are your "customers." In general, any one "downstream" from you is your customer.

A really good exercise for a staff meeting is to look at your organization's service (or your personal service to customers at a private meeting with yourself!) in terms of this grading schema. How "good" (really) is your service?

Conclusion

Managing jobs involves extracting the essential job from the humongous job description, attaching times and weights (effort ratio), and setting acceptable (better, best, and exceptional) levels of performance as a way to insure quality and movement toward quality. And finally, we have talked about ways to measure (or at least assess) quality using a customer/consumer satisfaction model.

Part 4 - Chapter 8

MANAGING TASKS

Introduction

After you have stepped on the supervisory ladder with supervisory management, you then move to project manager. As with each step up the managerial ladder, responsibility for the previous level is retained, except, now you are essentially managing projects. This step is more complex for three reasons.

1. The tasks are made up of collections of parts of jobs. You have to be aware of a greater range of elements.
2. Projects are similarly made up of bundles of assignments. In both cases a range of people and competencies are involved. They can be inside or outside the organization, above, below or beside you. Hence they have to be "orchestrated". That means, of course, that you know the score.
3. The reason this step is more complex is that you now have to be significantly more aware of external factors/events outside of your project that may affect your work. For example, these factors/events need to consider such factors as religious holidays that can affect scheduling.

Tasks / Projects / Orchestration

A project is an interrelated set of tasks designed to accomplish a mission. These tasks exist over time, and may involve a range of players. There are dates and deliverables for projects. An example of a project could be an annual meeting, a fund-raising event for an agency, the completion of an adoption process for a couple, the submission of a funding request to state government, or grant application to a community foundation. People, equipment, and jobs come together in tasks. Task bundles are assembled in batches, and then strung together to form a string of tasks, and when completed, result in the product (event, submission, whatever). Both bundles and batches need to be carefully managed.

The bundles need to be formed into coherent batches. These batches, in turn, sequenced appropriately so that the desired outcome (deliverable) can be achieved by the desired time (date). The term project is a way to refer to the whole package of task bundles, usually named after or referring to the end product, such as "Planning the Annual meeting." Orchestration addresses the managerial issue of ordering, sequencing, tempo, entrances and exits of parts, and elements, which all need to work synchronously in order for the product to be produced on time, in budget, and the outcome to be achieved. Orchestration is the process through which tasks coalesce into projects and achieve completion.

Parts and Elements

Tasks can be thought of as comprised of parts and elements. Parts are temporally and functionally discrete jobs. They start and finish at some point within the project process, and accomplish some subgoal (renting the hall, sending out invitations, etc.). They may actually reappear at various intervals throughout the project (quarterly budget checks), but they still start and stop. Elements of the project, on the other hand, are ongoing. They tend to occur throughout the process of the project (environmental scanning, etc.). Managers need to attend to both the episodic parts and ongoing elements of the project.

Events and Activities

A similar conceptualization pertains to events and activities. Events can be thought of as nodes in the project process, where one task bundled ends. You might also call that a milestone, such as "we have completed the first draft of our project proposal" or "all the paperwork for this international adoption had been finished." Activities connect events. Almost always there is a time period between the completion of one task bundle and the beginning of another task bundle. That interstitial period is an activity, where something is happening (or not happening!). Think of a project like a link of sausages. There are plump parts (the events) and the squeezed parts (the activities.).

Managing the Exceptions (Allocating Managerial Energy)

Managers need to be aware of the process, parts, elements, events, and activities that make up the typical project. Most projects in organizations are usual and (more or less) understood. They have a repetitive aspect to them in which "local knowledge" helps the employees to self-manage. Managers often make the mistake of "managing" (intruding on) processes, which are already running well, and failing to apply energy to areas of need. Generally, managers need to encourage the steady pace of the "routine and the regular" while, at the same time, "managing the exceptions." Each manager has somewhat different expectations for how the "routine and the regular" should function including pace, cost, and quality. Routine and regular processes do vary within these (and other) parameters, and addressing them is part (a big part) of the manager's job. Most quality problems come from system failures - problems and issues within the routine and the regular that have been unattended by managers. These are the exceptions, or special problems in ongoing processes that cause problems, often increasing problems downstream. Managing the exceptions means attending to smaller problems earlier in the process, if possible, so that they do not mushroom and, in addition to the problem itself, cause problems in other areas.

A project is like a small stream with sections in it. A branch (problem) removed causes no issue. If left to float downstream it often catches on something, and becomes a magnet for other branches (problems). Even if they are all small, taken together they can become a serious blockage. Similarly, in project management, problems will build upon each other. If dealt with in a timely fashion the project can proceed. If the problem is ignored, it begins to multiply, causing additional problems.

Ideas, Decisions, and Execution

Managing projects is a conceptual job, in the same sense that managing people is an interpersonal job. A manager needs to have ideas about the flow of the project. These ideas deal with sequences, likelihoods, blockages, chokepoints, interdependencies, and simultaneities. A manager also should have ideas about components. Will component C be ready when component B shows up? Then there are the externalities. What elements outside the project (other projects, for example) might get in the way? The manager needs to CONCEPTUALIZE the entire project and its components, much like an orchestra conductor conceptualizes an entire piece as well as all of its subparts, or as a chef conceptualizes a menu. Management is reactive of course, addressing the inevitable instances of Murphy's Law. Better management anticipates, but the best management is when you do not notice there is any management at all. The project (musical rendition, meal) is so seamless that it seems effortless; the best management pro-acts (See Figure 22).

Good, Better, and Best Management

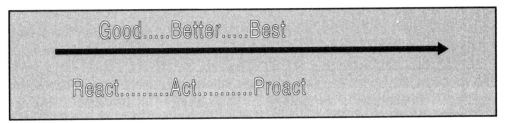

Figure 22

Based upon the conceptualization, managers then need to make decisions. We have all experienced the manager who seems to be unable to decide anything. They are below reaction, there seems to be a paralysis there, a "deer in the headlights" kind of thing. That is of course, an extreme case but not an unknown one. Then there is the pokey decision maker, who is "too little too late." A manager should, of course, want to avoid the opposite as well – the so called "Fire, Ready, Aim" approach. Decision pre-maturity is as bad as decision post-maturity.

And finally, managers have to execute. They have to make, cause, and arrange for things to actually happen. We sometimes divide people into two groups along these lines – people who seem to make things happen or those who do not. I am not talking managers here, though it is an essential managerial skill. Rather, I am referring to the people we know who, when they say they are going to invite you over, actually do invite you over; the people who say "let's vacation in the Adirondacks" and actually make the arrangements; the people who, when they say they are going to do something, pretty much anything, actually DO that something.

Executioners create results and outcomes, they actually achieve objectives. Execution is a skill different from conceptualization and decision making. It involves active engagement with the project (but not taking over the project) so that the project actually happens. While it sometimes involves doing things yourself, it more often evolves into doing a little bit of a lot of things, so that others are motivated to finish up. For example, your friend might not plan the entire trip to the Adirondacks, but might get some initial information that excites your interests; you then begin to work on planning the trip also. So executioners are initiators. Executioners are also a "right now" versus a "not now" type of person. They seem to prefer sooner, rather than later. This is because there is a flicker of interest and motivation about "it" which needs to be captured and propelled forward. That flicker is like the tiny flame in the logs of your fireplace. If there are the right twigs there, that single flame can catch a twig, then a large log, and so on. Execution is capturing and feeding that flicker and turning it into a fire of outcomes.

Schedule Control

One of the most important elements for the project manager is schedule control. Schedule control involves three basic skills:

1) seeing the project through conceptualization;
2) component time estimation;
3) writing both the components and time down for all to see.

Project conceptualization is the ability to see the whole project, event, dinner, or performance in its entirety. Conceptualization involves a manager who is able to see both the parts and the elements, the events and activities, which will be needed to make it succeed, as well as their sequences and interdependency. The second skill, component time estimation, simply involves a good sense of how long it will take to complete A so that we know when to schedule B, so that in turn we know when to schedule C, and so on. Both these skills involve not only knowing the event, but also the necessary activities that lead up to the event. The third element is, perhaps, not really a skill. It involves simply writing down and posting the "plan" so that all involved can know when their responsibilities are and the time frames in which they have to work. It is amazing how many project managers go through steps 1 and 2, and then fail to inform others of the "plan," so their work on steps 1 and 2 is essentially useless.

There are three main tools that you can use for the purpose of informing others of the "plan". One is Logic Modeling, two is Gantt charting, and three is PERT (Program Evaluation and Review Technique) charting. Before we move to those techniques, let me provide a checklist for achieving a useful schedule (Figure 23).

Techniques for Achieving a Useful Schedule

Developing Achievable Schedules (based on Project Mgt. For Dummies Cheat Sheet)
• Start with the end in mind (Covey, 1990) Be WHERE by WHEN?
• Identify all required events - an act or goal existing at a point in time
• Identify all required activities - a process existing over time which connects events
• Break activities /events down into sufficient detail
• Consider needed resources
• Perform an assumptions audit; record crucial assumptions
• Revisit your schedule regularly
• In minor ways
• In major ways
• Time estimate - how long a project component will take (Te or Time estimate) (Tm maximum time the component can take)
• Consider the other projects going on for your impact on them and theirs on you
• Develop Plans B and C for high-risk segments (the no-slack path: Te = Tm)

Figure 23

Improving Your Personal Estimates (based on Project Mgt. For Dummies Cheat Sheet)

- Distinguish between person effort and duration;

- Describe clearly all the work to be done on all activities

- Specify personnel requirements by skills and knowledge (competence)

- Revise your estimates, if necessary, after people have been assigned to your team

Logic Modeling/Dates and Deliverables

The key thing about logic modeling is an orderly progression from start to finish of the elements involved in a project. Usually the following elements are included:

inputs	processes outputs	short-term outcomes	intermediate outcomes	long-term outcomes[1]

[1]*See Example 1 A Logic Model on page 99 at the end of this chapter.*

Logic modeling represents a horizontal flow of project subtasks from the initiating task to the concluding task. Inputs include resources, customers, supplies, and other elements that start the project. Inputs would also include notes and records from previous iterations of the project. Processes address the operations that are performed on the inputs to produce outputs. Outputs in turn evolve into short-term and long-term outcomes.

Consider the adoption process as an example in logic modeling. Inputs consist of children and potential parents, as well as various resources and staff the agency might have (there are other routes to adoption other than a child welfare agency, but the child welfare agency is the focus here). Processes are the steps the agency creates for the child, the adoptive parents, and relevant others (natural mom, dad, etc) on the way to the adoption finalization. These may include visits, working out arrangements with the natural mom, etc. An output would be the finalization of the adoption. An outcome would be a positive result for parents and child. The short-term outcomes would be those that happen immediately after the adoption, such as adjustment in the first year; long-term outcomes might include the child growing up to be an adult who can love and work. Because so much has been written about logic models, I have included two especially good pieces as endpapers to this chapter. Each is available, as are others, on the web. For a detailed discussion (78 pages) you might wish to look at one of the Logic Model documents sponsored by the Kellogg Foundation also available on the web at http://www.wkkf.org/Pubs/Tools/Evaluation/Pub3669.pdf.

Gantt Charting

Once you have the logic model in mind, you can move on to Gantt charting. Gantt charting simply adds start, duration, and finish times to all the tasks that comprise the processes phase (but can also apply to outputs and outcomes).

Organizations require managerial supervisors to again ask themselves: What do you need and when do you need it? Once a supervisor answers these questions then they can begin to list and compile resources needed to meet the milestones. The Gantt chart provides a visual tool for managerial supervisors to track what task will be going on during each phase of the journey towards the goal. The first example (Figure 24) shows that Task A will be a beginning task that ends prior to the completion of the goal whereas; Task C will run almost the entire time. Task D, in this example, will only occur in the completion stage. This example (Figure 24) is taken from everyday life and depicts how the goal of purchasing a new car can be divided up into four general tasks. Before you know what to buy you have to first know what you can afford to buy, which in this case is determined during the first month of the process. Task C, negotiating with dealers and lenders, is part of months 2-4, as it is an integral and ongoing part of the goal of buying a car.

Buying a New Car Example

	1	2	3	4
A. Calculate budget	■			
B. Research and test drive		■	■	
C. Negotiate		■	■	■
D. Financing and Purchasing				■
Month	1	2	3	4

Figure 24

Gantt charting, when used by child welfare supervisors, can be used to make planned decisions, such as case assignments, in a manner that prevents taxing workers beyond their skills, prevents possible work overloads, and assures agency time frames and mandates are met (see Figure 25).

Child Welfare Example: Making New Case Assignments

Are new cases emergencies?	▓			
Current worker caseloads		▓		
Worker skill level/new case complexity		▓	▓	
Assigning cases to workers				▓
Hour	**1**	**2**	**3**	**4**

Figure 25

Below is an example of the use of a Gantt chart for the supervisor. In this instance, it lays out a procedure for managerial supervisors who are assigning new cases. This is because every task is assigned to a time frame, which allows managers/supervisors to answer the questions "What do we need?" and "When do we need it?"

The managerial supervisor in child welfare can use Gantt charting with workers for each case on their caseload. When the supervisor sits down with the worker, the Gantt chart review is an excellent way for them to mutually chart case tasks, to assess case progress, and where simultaneity of activities lies and in what time frames. If the Gantt chart is employed with individual cases, there will be commonalities among tasks and time frames, although the needs of individual families and children must be taken into account. A sample blank Gantt template appears as Figure 26.

Blank Gantt Template

Task				
A				
B				
C				
D				
E				
Time Frame	1	2	3	4

Figure 26

PERT Charting

PERT, which stands for Program, Evaluation and Review Technique, is a way to identify and track project activities over time. Key concepts in PERT charting include the following:

- Events and Activities
- Predecessor and Successor Events; Simultaneous Events.
- Time Estimation: Activities have a Te = expected time an activity will take; and a Tm = maximum time an activity will take
- Critical Path is where Te=Tm
- When Te (is less than) < Tm you have Slack

Basically, a PERT chart is the next step after the Gantt chart. In Gantt charts you have actually developed a list of Events and Activities, although you might not have called it that. An <u>event</u> is an action occurring at a point in time; an <u>activity</u> is an action occurring over time. In the Gantt chart, Activities are represented by a bar. Shorter bar length means shorter activities, longer bar length means longer activities. Every Activity has two Events associated with it – an Initiating Event and a Terminal Event. The Event is the point where the bar begins (Initiating Event) and where the bar ends (Terminating Event).

As in the Gantt, in the PERT chart Events have a sequence, which needs to be followed so that the project can be completed. The first step in a PERT chart (which has largely been completed through the construction of a Gantt) is to make a two-column list of the Events and Activities needed to complete the project. Often it is good to use Post-its™ (one Event and one Activity on each Post it-™) so that the time order of Events and Activities can be easily changed. Often, as we review the initial time order of project Events and Activities, we see that we have them wrong, or that it would be helpful to do something earlier (or later) than we had originally thought, and we need to change the order of Events and Activities. Using Post-its™ makes it easy to do so. Simultaneous Events means that Events are "stacked" (two Events are occurring at the same time). In that case, two Activities may have different Initiating Events but the same Terminating Event.

The next phase of PERTing, is to lay out your Activities and Events across a time line, again much like in a Gantt. In PERT charts, you use a line instead of a bar to represent Activities. Above each line, in about the middle, there is a little symbol, Te =, which stands for "estimated time equals." The number following the = sign is the estimated time it will take to complete the Activity, and corresponds to the amount of space the line occupies on the base time line below. Below the line is another calculation, Tm =, which indicates the MAXIMUM amount of time the Activity can take. For example, suppose you were driving from Smithville to Greenston and takes it about 1 hour and you need to be there by 4PM for a meeting. If you leave at 2:30PM you could arrive 1/2 hour early, all going well. In this case Te>Tm. If you leave at 3PM exactly, Te=Tm. If you leave at 3:15PM then Te<Tm. In the first case, you have "slack" or extra time to play with in case something comes up. In the second case, you have the so-called "critical path" or no-slack path. In the third case, you have "crisis" because you have started too late and really have no chance of making the meeting, and might be tempted to use potentially problematic approaches (speeding, corner cutting) to make the meeting.

Below is an example of a Gantt and PERT for preparing Thanksgiving dinner.

Gantt Chart of Preparing Thanksgiving Dinner

	9-10	10-11	11-12	12-1	1-2
1) Put in Turkey	xxxxxx	xxxxxx	xxxxxx	xxxxxx	
2) Prepare Vegetables		xxxxxx			
3) Prepare Dessert		xxxxxx			
4) Check Turkey				xxxxxx	
5) Cook Vegetables				xxxxx	
6) Cook Dessert				xxxxx	
7) Set Table			xxxxxx		
8) Prepare Relish Tray					xxxxx
9) Remove Turkey				xxxxxx	
10) Assemble				xxxxxx	
11) EAT					Eat!!!!!

Microsoft Project will do Gantting and Perting. It is a little tough to learn, but would be worth it if you are doing a lot of this kind of work.

Figure 27

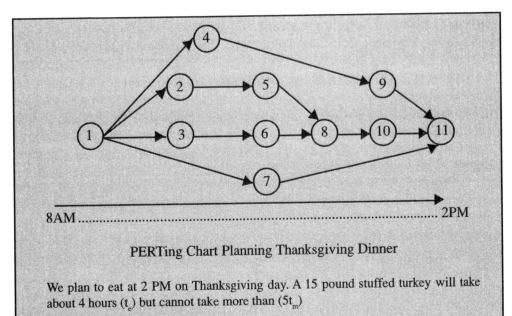

PERTing Chart Planning Thanksgiving Dinner

We plan to eat at 2 PM on Thanksgiving day. A 15 pound stuffed turkey will take about 4 hours (t_e) but cannot take more than ($5t_m$)

1. Put Turkey in Oven
   (t_e-4 hours; t_m-5 hours)
2. Prepare Vegetables
3. Prepare Dessert
4. Check Turkey
5. Cook Vegetables
6. Cook Dessert
7. Set Table
8. Prepare Relish Tray
9. Remove Turkey
10. Assemble Meal
11. Eat

These examples are pretty simple. A more detailed, but brief, explanation can be found at metmba.com. [http://www.metma.com/operations/project/PERT]

Some Tips for Task and Project Management

There are a lot of specific, useful things the supervisor, project manager and middle manager need to be aware of when it comes to task and project management. I have used a list from Project Management for Dummies (Portny, 2000) and added some explanations to some of their points where the meaning might not be self-evident (as suggested by students and supervisors with whom I have worked). These are just useful to keep in mind. (Portny has 6 areas in the Cheat sheet, a heavy paper tear-out in the front of the book. They are: Avoiding Common Pitfalls, Developing Meaningful Business Objectives, Developing Achievable Schedules, Improving Your Personal Estimates, Eliciting and Sustaining Commitment, and Communicating Effectively. Each area contains a set of bullets that alert managers to issues. I have selected Pitfalls, Objective and Eliciting and Sustaining Commitment as most relevant here.)

Avoiding Common Project Problems

Most tasks bundles and projects run into trouble because of the common, rather than the uncommon, issues and problems. A few are listed below:

#	Porty's Issue (Avoiding the Most Common Project Pitfalls)	Tropman's Suggestions
1	• Vague Objectives –	nail these down.
2	• Vague/Missing Assumptions –	do an assumptions audit.
3	• Key Commitments Not in Writing –	tough to do, but essential.
4	• Key Audiences Overlooked –	review the list of stakeholders to assure full coverage.
5	• Lack of Team-Member Commitment	– be sure to outline commitment requirements and changes in them, initially and as you go along.
6	• Failure to Hold People Accountable	– if they cannot/do not deliver, they lack integrity and should move along.
7	• Backing into Project Schedules	– letting the situations drive the schedules rather than developing them at the front end.
8	Failure to Define and Sustain a Team Identity	give your team a name!
9	• Insufficient Monitoring	inspect what you expect.
10	• No Formal Risk Identification and Management	attend to the critical paths (see PERT above; ask where things could really crash.
11	• Poor Communications	overcommunicate; use writing and verbal vehicles.
12	• No Organized Method For Introducing and Evaluation Requested Changes –	have a method for addressing suggestions for changes, deciding whether to adopt them, and outline procedures for implementing the changes in project flow and associated documents.
13	• Failure to Learn From the Past Project Lessons for the Next One	complete an "after action report" and "lessons learned document."

Developing Meaningful Objectives

As the common phrase has it, "If you do not know where you are going, any road will take you there." Crisp understandable objectives are crucial

#	Portny's Issues (Developing Meaningful Project Objectives)	Tropman's sugestions
1	Focus on Outcomes Rather Than Activities	Outcomes, rather than activities or outputs, are the name of the game; outcomes would be client improvement, for example, rather than interviews held; jobs secured for clients rather than referrals made; customer/client/consumer satisfaction rather than meetings.
2	• Use Clear Language	Obfuscatory polysyllabic verbiage need to be replaced with clear one-syllable words.
3	• Make Sure That Every Objective Has At Least One Measure	**Measures** are things like miles per hour, satisfaction scores, # of contacts in a week, # clients seen a day, and so on.
4	• Make Sure Every Measure Has at Least One Performance Target	**Performance targets** are minimal outcomes that the measure needs to achieve, such as miles per day completed, a certain number of clients per day, a certain number of weekly contacts, etc.
5	• Make Sure Every Objective Is Time Specific	As seen in the above two points, metrics and performance targets need to have times attached to them. These can be rates, or dates, but without time specificity, completion trajectories tend to recede.
6	• Make Sure It Is Possible To Achieve Each Objective	Realism is crucial in setting outcomes. Usually "stretch" objectives are ok (what you did before plus a little.) Once outcomes become impossible - they are seen as a tool of managment to speed up the line and stimulate gaming the system and lying and cheating.
7	• Check With all Project Drivers To Be Sure That You Have Identified All Their Expectations	Most projects have different people doing different things which periodcally come together only to separate again. Keep talking with those individuals so that they can share their issues with you.

Eliciting and Sustaining Commitment

Motivation and commitment to a project is something that, to some extent, workers bring to the job. People come to work for nonprofits because they believe in and are passionate about the mission that organization embodies, whether it is children's services or band, art or dance camp. However, commitment is like a houseplant - it may arrive healthy but it needs to be cared for and sustained. Managers need to be a "constant gardener" of that commitment, freeing it from weeds and providing it with nourishment.

#	Porty's Issue Eliciting and Sustaining Commitment	Tropman's Suggestions
1	Clarify How Your Project Will Benefit Agency/Firm Team Members	Constantly discuss the relationship between larger goals and personal ones.
2	• Involve Team Members in Process Planning	Involvement in problem solving brings technical solutions faster and builds emotional satisfaction.
3	• Demonstrate/Explain The Plan Feasibility	Part Fact Part Faith, this is the role of the project leader. Encouragement plus practicality. The metrics developed above will help.
4	• Address Issues, Concerns, Questions Promptly and Openly	Regular meetings that identify issues to be resolved, workarounds to be constructed, decisions to be made will help rather than "newsletter reporting."
5	Provide Frequent and Meaningful Feedback On Project Status	Use meetings for problem sharing, and feedback securing. Involve all the team in Feedback Sessioin.
6	Recognize People's Contributions	Have a team "ego wall." This can be an overall measure like the thermometer that United Way uses during its campaign, as well as acheivements of the subunits. Celebratory emails to the team are also useful.
7	Encourage Team Members to Get to Know One Another	Host informal events for the team.
8	Focus on People's Strengths Rather Than Their Limitations	Worry less about what is "left out," strengthen what is "left in."

Enhancing People's Performance

- Host a Variety Of Informal Team Social Events for the Team

	• Recognize People's Contributions	
	• Encourage Team Members To Get To Know Each Other • Focus On People's Strengths Rather Than Their Limitations	

Conclusion

The task and project manager develops two sets of skills in terms of the project itself. One is task assembly, sequencing and orchestration. The second is execution.

Task assembly involves putting together the relevant parts of jobs into task bundles, and then ordering the bundles so that their completion, one after the other, leads to project completion, within the parameters of time and budget. The process of accomplishing, bundling, and sequencing is called orchestration.

The manager also needs to conceptualize the project (have ideas about it) so that there is an overarching frame of reference into which elements and parts fit. Decisions about problems and potential problems need to be made in a timely manner. And once those decisions are made, there needs to be execution – the part that actually makes things happen. The very best managers are always a step ahead; their presence is unnoticed because the product is so good. Making things happen, or helping things to happen, or encouraging things to happen is a skill unto itself. We all know lots of people who have great plans but can never bring anything to fruition. We also know people who make things happen but they are often the wrong things.

Example 1: A Logic Model
Guidelines and Framework for
Designing Basic Logic Model
by *Carter McNamara, MBA, PhD*
http://www.managementhelp.org/np_progs/np_mod/org_frm.htm

Description

The following framework can be filled in by readers to design a logic model (or diagram) for their organization and for each of its programs. Guidelines and examples are provided to help the reader.

Purpose of a Logic Model

A logic model is a top-level depiction the flow of materials and processes to produce the results desired by the organization or program. The model can be very useful to organize planning and analysis when designing the organization and its programs or when designing outcomes-based evaluations of programs. It can also be useful for describing organizations and programs (for example, in grant proposals).

What to Include and What Not to Include

Logic models can be in regard to whatever application in which the designer chooses to use them. However, when using logic models to analyze or describe organizations and programs, it's often best to use logic models to depict major, recurring items in the organization or programs -- rather than one-time items. For example, you might not choose to do a logic model for the one-time, initial activities to build an organization or program (constructing the building, registering with state and federal authorities, etc.). However, you might benefit more from using logic models to analyze and describe the major, recurring activities that occur in the organization or program (once they're built) to continue to produce the results desired for clients and the community.

Size and Level of Detail

The logic model should be of a size that readers can easily study the model without extensive reference and cross-comparisons between pages. Ideally, the logic model is one or at most two pages long. The level of detail should be sufficient for the reader to grasp the major items that go into an organization or program, what occurs to those inputs, the various outputs that results and the overall benefits/impacts (or outcomes) that occur and to which groups of people.

Note the content of program logic models is often more specific than models for organizations. This level of specificity is often quite useful for program planners.

Definitions of Basic Terms

Logic models typically depict the inputs, processes, outputs and outcomes associated with an organization and its programs. Don't be concerned about your grasping the "correct" definition of each of the following terms. It's more important to have some sense of what they mean -- and even more important to be consistent in your use of the terms.

Inputs

These are materials that the organization or program takes in and then processes to produce the results desired by the organization. Types of inputs are people, money, equipment, facilities, supplies, people's ideas, people's time, etc. Inputs can also be major forces that influence the organization or programs. For example, the inputs to a nonprofit program that provides training to clients might include learners, training materials, teachers, classrooms, funding, paper and pencils, etc. Various laws and regulations effect how the program is conducted, for example, safety regulations, Equal Opportunity Employment guidelines, etc. Inputs are often associated with a cost to obtain and use the item -- budgets are listings of inputs and the costs to obtain and/or use them.

Processes (or Activities or Strategies or Methods)

Processes are used by the organization or program to manipulate and arrange items to produce the results desired by the organization or program. Processes can range from putting a piece of paper on a desk to manufacturing a space shuttle. However, logic models are usually only concerned with the major recurring processes associated with producing the results desired by the organization or program. For example, the major processes used by a nonprofit program that provides training to clients might include recruitment of learners, pretesting of learners, training, post-testing and certification.

Outputs

Outputs are usually the tangible results of the major processes in the organization. They are usually accounted for by their number, for example, the number of students who failed or passed a test, courses taught, tests taken, teachers used, etc. Outputs are frequently misunderstood to indicate success of an organization or program. However, if the outputs aren't directly associated with achieving the benefits desired for clients, and then the outputs are poor indicators of the success of the organization and its programs. You can use many teachers, but that won't mean that many clients were successfully trained.

Outcomes

Outcomes are the (hopefully positive) impacts on those people whom the organization wanted to benefit with its programs. Outcomes are usually specified in terms of:
a) learning, including enhancements to knowledge, understanding/perceptions/attitudes, and behaviors
b) skills (behaviors to accomplish results, or capabilities)
c) conditions (increased security, stability, pride, etc.)

It's often to specify outcomes in terms of short-term, intermediate and long-term.

Basic Example of a Logic Model

The following example is intended to further portray the nature of inputs, processes, outputs and outcomes.

The logic model is for an organization called the Self-Directed Learning Center (SDLC).

Logic models for programs are often more detailed. Note that the more comprehensive and descriptive your logic model

inputs	processes	outputs	short-term outcome(s)	intermediate outcomes	long-term outcomes
- Free articles and other publications on the Web - Collaborators - Free Management Library - Funders - Self-directed learners· - Volunteers - Computers - Web - Supplies	- Provide peer-assistance models in which learners support each other - Provide free, on-line training program: Basics of Self-Directed Learning - Provide free, on-line training program: Basic Life Skills - Provide free, on-line training program: Passing your GED Exam	- 30 groups that used peer models - 100 completed training programs - 900 learners who finished Basics of Self-Directed Learning - 900 learners who finished Basic Life Skills - 900 learners who passed their GED to gain high-school diploma	- high school diploma for graduates - improved attitude toward self and society for graduates - improved family life for family of graduates	- full-time employment for learners (in job that required high-school education) - increased reliability and improved judgment of learners - enhanced publicity and public relations for SDLC	- independent living for learner (by using salary to rent apartment) - strong basic life skills for learner - improved love life for learner who's now in a relationship - increased likelihood and interest for learner to attend college

Logic Model
for

Organization (Name)

_____

Or Program (Name)

_____

inputs	processes	outputs	short-term outcomes	intermediate outcomes	long-term outcomes

Used by The Management Assistance Program for Nonprofits
2233 University Avenue West, Suite 360
St. Paul, Minnesota 55114 (651) 647-1216
With permission from Carter McNamara, MBA, PhD, Copyright 2000

Example 2

Everything You Wanted to Know About Logic Models But Were Afraid to Ask

Connie C. Schmitz, Professional Evaluation Services, Minneapolis, MN

Beverly A. Parsons, InSites, Boulder, CO

http://www.insites.org/documents/logmod.htm

This paper was funded by the W.K. Kellogg Foundation (WKKF) under a contract to InSites, a Colorado-based nonprofit 501(c)3 organization. The information and opinions provided herein are the sole responsibility of the authors and do not represent agreement or positions of WKKF. Not for attribution or citation without permission from WKKF or InSites.

EVERYTHING YOU WANTED TO KNOW ABOUT LOGIC MODELS BUT WERE AFRAID TO ASK

This paper addresses situations where a private foundation designs an initiative and awards grants to a number of sites to participate in the initiative in their local setting. The basic ideas are applicable to other situations.

What is a Logic Model?

The term "logic model" comes from the evaluation field, but these models don't just belong to evaluators or the evaluation plan. As the term suggests, they are a basic element of programming that communicates the logic behind a program, its rationale. A logic model's purpose is to communicate the underlying "theory" or set of assumptions or hypotheses that program proponents have about why the program will work, or about why it is a good solution to an identified problem.

Logic models are typically diagrams, flow sheets, or some other type of visual schematic that conveys relationships between contextual factors and programmatic inputs, processes, and outcomes. Logic models can come in all shapes and sizes: boxes with connecting lines that are read from left to right (or top to bottom); circular loops with arrows going in or out; or other visual metaphors and devices. What these schemata have in common are they attempt to show the links in a chain of reasoning about "what causes what," in relationship to the desired outcome or goal. The desired outcome or goal is usually shown as the last link in the model.

How are Logic Models Different from Action Plans?

Logic models are often confused with "action plans." While there are some overlaps, the difference is subtle but very important. An action plan is a manager's guide for running the project. It shows, often through a set of program objectives and a time line or task outline, what staff or others need to do to implement a project (e.g., "hire out-reach worker," "launch media campaign," "revise curricula"). A logic model illustrates the presumed effects of hiring an outreach worker, launching a media campaign, or using revised curricula. (For example, "trained outreach workers lead to more information about AIDS getting dispensed in a high-risk neighborhood; increased contacts with outreach workers leads to a greater proportion of hard-to-reach clients coming in for treatment"). These hypotheses about program effects are described in a logic model, are tested in a "theory-based" evaluation, and lead to "lessons learned." If program planners don't have any hypotheses guiding them, their potential for learning from the initiative is low, and the program is probably in trouble.

Why develop Logic Models?

Logic models are useful for all parties involved in an initiative—the initiating organization's board members and top administrators, initiative leaders and staff, participating organizations, evaluators, and others seeking to understand the work. Logic models:

- *convey the fundamental purpose of an initiative*

- *show why the initiative is important*

- *show what will result from an initiative*

- *depict the actions/causes expected to lead to the desired results*

- *become a common language and reference point for everyone involved in the initiative*

- *serve as the basis to determine whether planned actions are likely to lead to the desired results*

How Detailed Should Logic Models Be?

Ideally a logic model is contained within a single page with enough detail that it can be explained fairly easily and understood by other people. The value of a logic model is that it visually expresses beliefs about why the program is likely to succeed. Because it is visual, it typically can be more easily remembered. If the model has so much detail, however, or is so complexly drawn that is cannot be remembered, it loses some of its value. On the other hand, if the model is so stripped of information that it consists of just a few abstract headings or generic looking boxes, then it may not communicate the program's logic well enough to be useful.

A logic model may be divided into key parts or phases with each part/phase on a separate page. The parts would be accompanied by a less detailed full model given on one page that shows how the parts fit together into a whole.

Logic modeling is an art than requires practice!

How Else Can Program Logic Be Conveyed?

Logic models represent a visual way of expressing the rationale or thought behind a program. Two other forms of expression may help concurrently support the development of a logic model, or accompany the model if it is to be communicated through written materials.

One form is a short narrative that explains in words why this program is believed to be successful. A good narrative does the same thing as the logic model, but it may be more clear or persuasive, especially if it conveys the program planners' deep understanding of "the problem," or a passionate argument about why certain strategies or actions are believed efficacious. A narrative can also communicate a programming philosophy or ethic that a visual model cannot.

A second form is a set of "if-then" statements. These statements, which are written out as a set of short bulleted phrases, are unabashedly analytic. "If such and such can be achieved or is allowed to happen . . . then such and such will follow. And if such and such follows, then we should see some decrease in the problem which we are address-ing, or increase in the type of outcome we're looking for." Good "if-then" statements help supply some of the detail missing in a logic model; they attempt to fill in as many of the critical "links in the chain of reasoning" as possible.

What are Logic Models Based On?

Logic models are based on knowledge about a field of endeavor that can be gained from personal and professional experience, the research literature, background infor-mation from key informants, future projections, and other sources. It's difficult to de-velop a logic model, however—or a narrative rationale, or the "if-then" statements—without clearly defining a need and developing a deep understanding of the problem. As a philosopher of science once said, "The seeds of every solution are embedded in the formulation of the problem."

Faulty logic models occur when the essential problem has not been clearly stated and defined, or factors influencing a problem are not well understood. It's not enough to have a goal (although clear goals are also essential). Goals exist because some action is needed. And it's hard to argue that action is needed if you don't have a problem. The factors affecting problems (and therefore goals) include both positive influences (called "protective factors" in some fields) as well as negative influences ("risk factors"). De-veloping a "mental map of the problem" is therefore a crucial preliminary step to devel-oping a logic model and formulating a program strategy. These mental models of the problem can also be diagrammed in a visual way to show the causal effects of variables on outcomes. A good logic model will show how the initiative is strategically address-ing factors that influence the problem. If the logic model is unrelated to the mental map of the problem, then that signals a "red flag" either in the conceptualization of the problem, or in the programming strategy.

Who gets involved in developing logic models?

The development of a logic model begins with the initiative developers, e.g., a founda-tion. Their theory of "cause and effect" is the basis for the model. They may involve planners or evaluators with experience in logic modeling to help convert their theory into a logic model.

Once the initiative has a logic model, participants in the initiative (e.g., grantees of the foundation) develop their own more specific logic model that is congruent with the initiative's model. Their model may show the role of the organization leading the initia-tive.

When should logic models be developed, revised, or changed?

A foundation initiative typically would have a logic model in its initial description. However, foundation initiatives involve ongoing learning. Thus the initial logic model may need to be revised periodically. One likely time for revisions would be when grantees develop their site-specific models. During that process, new information may arise that suggests a need for revisions of the initial model. Other likely revision times are at the end of each phase of an initiative or at major evaluation reporting points.

Should the foundation be a defined entity within a logic model?

The answer to this question may vary depending on what the foundation's role is. A foundation can be a significant force—money, credibility, people, knowledge—in the success of the work during the life of the grant. If ownership and initiation of the initiative comes largely from the foundation at the beginning and needs to move to the sites, it may be important to explicitly show this transition in the model.

Part 4 - Chapter 9

MANAGING WORK

Introduction

While supervisory management addresses the concerns of *jobs*, the project management addresses matters pertaining to *tasks*, and the middle management produces *work*. **Work** is a set of projects that, as they are collectively successful, accomplish the mission of the organization and embody and articulate its *raison d'etre* or purpose. Work must also embody the core values of the organization in such a way that the goals are produced, but produced through acceptable means. For example, if an organization is set up to serve the poor, and does so, but pays substandard wages to their own employees, we have a situation of exploiting one group to help another exploited group. While outcomes may be achieved, the means are unacceptable (exploitation of staff) and hence become diminished and questionable. Middle management is more concerned with effectiveness (doing the right things, in the right way) than efficiency (doing things right).

So, the middle manager has the added responsibilities of integrating projects, but doing so, in a mindful way that weighs competing and useful projects on higher planes of priorities. Resources of money and people are deducted from here and added to there, in line with the overall mission of the organization. The middle manager's job is a conscious dance among competing values. Take McDonalds for example (or any fast food chain), they have two products (at least), one is "fast" and the other is "food". There is a constant need to balance the demands of these two products on a daily basis. To make things a little more complex, let's take three variables – faster, better, and cheaper. Managers of work processes are continually juggling these three variables – how can we work more quickly, how can we work at higher levels of quality, and how can we work less expensively?

And these conflicts do not take into account the larger issues within American society that permeate the organization such as achievement versus equality, air play versus fair share, ethnic, gender, racial and sexual preference divisions which crosscut our culture. Managers must keep their eyes on the prize, but also on conflicts, footfalls, slippery slopes, and many other issues that get in the way of achieving that prize. For human service organizations, one of the most important conflicts might be called mission versus margin.

Managing Work: Mission versus Margin

The term Mission refers to the provision of help and assistance to those who need it. This is a core value of any human service organization. Other organizations may have other missions than providing help, but all organizations have some mission. The term Margin refers to financial stability and profit. It is the manager's job (as well as the CEO and Board) to be sure that mission is key and it drives the margin, not the other way around. That does not mean that margin does not act as an important boundary. You cannot perform services for which you are not paid, or for which your pay (as occurs in many government contracts) is unilaterally reduced. It also means, that you do not do services which are not in your mission just because they have margin.

Wicked Problems

Doing work in the human services is one of the most difficult organizations in which to be employed. There are several reasons for this difficulty. I have already outlined a number of them in chapter 3 on the nonprofit and human service organization. Below is a recap of that list for easy reference (as listed in Figure 28).

Rittel and Weber's List Recapped

1. There is no definitive formulation of a wicked problem
2. Wicked problems have no stopping rule
3. Solutions to wicked problems are not true or false, but good or bad
4. There is no immediate and no ultimate test of a solution to a wicked problem
5. Every solution to a wicked problem is a "one-shot operation"; because there is no opportunity to learn by trial and error, every attempt counts significantly
6. Wicked problems have an innumerable (rather than an exhaustible describable) set of potential solutions; there is not a well-described set of permissible operations that may be incorporated into the plan
7. Every wicked problem is essentially unique
8. Every wicked problem can be considered a symptom of another problem
9. The existence of a discrepancy representing a wicked problem can be explained in numerous ways. The choice of explanation determines the nature of the problem's resolution
10. The manager has no right to be wrong

Figure 28

Adding to this set of pressures, however, there is the presence of higher expectations of non-profit executives, relating to the service purpose of their mission. The higher purpose or civic purpose of an organizations (nonprofit social service agencies, churches, philanthropies, etc.), may create a stress of its own. Somehow you hope that organizations established to serve the community and to help others, organizations set up to offer religious services, and so on, would hold to a higher standard. These higher expectations are problematic in their own right. In addition, these may add even **more** problems because their stakeholders, tending to think of nonprofits and their staff as more pure than corporate executives, and less vulnerable to the range of human venalities available It is likely that nonprofit executives and boards have this view of themselves. If so, the staff and governance structure should be less robust and have fewer social/organizational controls which need, apparently, to be always in place and always working.

Another part of this package might be the assumption, perhaps driven by the early domination of human service agencies by volunteers, and their current strong and important presence, that staff members are sort of "volunteers" too. I cannot tell readers how many times I have heard the phrase (in my own School of Social Work as well as many others), "You do not go into human services to make money." While there is a certain truth to this (other motivations are perhaps dominant) the need for a living wage does not go away. And the phrase is often used to excuse asking for appropriate compensation.

In my own case, as an example, I was once interviewed for a deanship of a School of Social Work at a University in the Eastern United States. After two days of meetings, the matter of compensation had still not been brought up. I thought I should initiate some conversation about this, and asked the woman who was chair of the search committee (and also President of the Board of Directors) what they were thinking of in terms of compensation. This woman (one of those who could enlarge herself while sitting completely still) commented, "Well, Doctor, at this University, you do not get rich, you get enriched." This mindset is still very prevalent. (By the way, I did not get the offer and was told I was too "pushy" for the culture at that time.)

Staff Accomplishment and Product Production

I recognize the complexities (and could outline many others) for human services managers to recognize the difficulties and stresses under which they labor. That said, there is still the need to assure both accomplishment and product. I use these two terms because, for the successful organization, they must occur together.

The product is the actual service outcome that the agency seeks to deliver. That can be mental health, sobriety, adoption, more highly functional individuals and families, nutritious meals for the poor, etc. The actual creation of service outcomes is the results of jobs, tasks, and projects coming together regularly, over time. People involved are not only the actual service providers, but also the service enablers (finance, audit, secretarial and office support, etc.).

Product production must be seamless, regular, dependable, and accountable. Much of what the manager actually does (captured in the phrase managing by wandering around or MBWA) involves a constant touching of bases and "howz-it-going?" queries. The manager is constantly meeting with not only project managers, but managerial supervisors as well. As the manager meets with the project managers, questions come up that can be addressed now or later, after reflection and checking. If issues come up with supervisors, the manager checks back with the relevant project manager and lets the project manager get back to the supervisor.

Along with these activities, the managers are managing "out" - checking and clearing with community and other agency stakeholders for important and relevant information. This activity is both a sharing "out" and a bringing "in" of information. Similarly, the manager is managing "up," checking in with the CEO or other members of the top team.

The manager is working "along with" the product teams and workers (but is not micromanaging). The manager is also in a "feed forward" mode, using current information (from MBWA) plus experience (distilled information from history) to work forward – ahead of the product flow, to clear potential obstacles. And of course managers also sometimes play "cleanup" as well, working behind the product flow to repair, assuage, and generally deal with hurt feelings, stakeholders that were overlooked, etc.

However, product assurance is only one of the two big jobs of the manager. The other is accomplishment assurance. Accomplishment is some thing that the staff needs to feel and experience. They need appreciation, thanks, recognition, and a constantly vitalized sense of their own importance in the delivery of product. So often, workers in any industry feel unappreciated and unrecognized. Delivering product with a demoralized staff is a sign of managerial failure. And in fact, a demoralized (as opposed to an energized) staff cannot deliver quality product. On the other hand, a staff that feels really good about themselves, but does not actually do anything, will not feel good for long. Of course, accomplishment creation is even more vital in organizations like human service agencies, which deal with the pressure of human difficulty and also experience "wicked problems" on a daily basis.

One element managers need to be especially aware of is the need to deal with under performing individuals. Everyone at work (and we know this to be true from our own experience) knows that there are those within the workforce who are not only not doing their share, but also are off-loading work on others. Almost nothing sours workers on their workplace more than to see these individuals consistently "getting away" with this behavior, and even more infuriating, getting rewarded at the same rate of pay! There is no question this is a tough job for managers. But it is not possible to produce accomplishment and the good feelings that both engender and result from accomplishment while supporting workplace laggards. It is time for them to move along!

Conclusion

Managers need to integrate task bundles into work products which flow out of the agency on a regular basis. They need to work not only with the service providers but also with the service enablers. Through MBWA, managers should try to be in constant familiarity with what the staff (supervisory managers and project managers) is contending with. Additionally, managers should also be looking to the community, peers in and out of the organization, and the CEO to both receive information and to get information they can pass along.

Part 5

MANAGERIAL LEVELS: Issues and Techniques in Supervisory, Project and Middle Management

Introduction

As one moves up the Managerial Staircase from worker to managerial supervisor, from managerial supervisor to project manager, and from project manager to middle manager, we note problems and issues at each level. For purposes here, I am going to draw upon the work of Buckingham and Coffman, from the Gallup Organization in their important book, "First Break All the Rules" (1999). The title really invites us to break one rule – treat everyone the same. Management is a customizing profession. While there is a lot in common what one does as any kind of manager, there is also a lot of unique application as well. Management might be thought of, in the words of Stan Davis, as "mass customization" (1987, 1996). Davis asserts that one has a basic managerial template, which is customized to the "managee" (down, over, across, up, and out). Davis uses the example of a shirt manufacturer to illustrate his point. This shirt manufacturer has your shirt or blouse sizes stored, then when you order, the manufacturer can add colors, sleeves, monograms, etc. as you wish. The mass part is the standard part; the customization part is adjusting the template of the product to your unique wishes at some point in time, thus creating "mass customization". Management is a lot like that. I like the approach in the Rules Book because it corresponds with one I have been independently developing on reward systems, and was published in my book, "The Compensation Solution" (Tropman, 2002). But more on that later. Let's first look at the Rules.

The book "First Break All the Rules" interviewed about two million workers, asking them questions about that job, and their likes and dislikes in their job. After processing their data (there are interesting methodological discussions in the appendices to their book for those who seek more information), they discovered there were twelve elements or dimensions, framed as questions to be answered, that characterized the very best managerial situations. They are listed in Figure 29 on the next page. While the authors did not look at them in terms of a Managerial Staircase, I feel that they fit nicely into our three-step set of levels. The authors had a slightly different grouping having four categories – Base Camp (What do I get?), Camp 1 (What do I give?), Camp 2 (Do I belong Here?) and Camp 3 (How Can We All Grow?). Note my slight reorganization is in Figure 29.

The 12 Questions that Characterize the Best Managerial Situations

Base Camp - Managerial Supervisors [What Do I Get?]

1] Do I know what is expected of me at work?

2] Do I have the materials and equipment to do my work right?

3] At work, do I have the opportunity every day to do what I do best?

Mid Camp - Project Managers [What Do I Give?]

4] In the last seven days, have I received recognition or praise for doing good work?

5] Does my supervisor, or someone at work, seem to care about me as a person?

6] Is there someone at work who encourages my development?

7] At work, do my opinions seem to count?

The Penultimate - Middle Mangers [Do I Belong Here? and Can We All Grow?]

8] Does the mission/purpose of my company make me feel my job is important?

9] Are my coworkers committed to doing quality work?

10] Do I have a best friend at work?

11] In the last six months, has someone at work talked to me about my progress?

12] This past year, have I had the opportunity to learn and grow?

Figure 29

Their packaging is a little different from the one used here, but the order is the same. I begin with the job, move to the tasks, and conclude with the work. Readers will notice that the questions (or focal issues) increase in number with each level. Managerial supervisors (Base Camp) are primarily concerned with thee questions, project managers (Mid Camp) with 4, and middle managers (The Penultimate) with 5. Since the managerial enterprise is additive, middle managers have a tough job, and the most to do; that is why they are paid (or not) the big bucks. You might ask why middle managers are listed as the "penultimate" (they call it the summit). My sense is that the ultimate task or focal issue is bringing everything together – the top team (the level above middle managers, and including the CEO) is the coordinating group that does what needs to be done. They might focus on any of the 12 – whatever is lacking in the organization. It could be big or small, but it is necessary for the organization to prosper. The 12 questions as listed in Figure 29 will be discussed in the next Chapter.

There are a couple of issues that affect each and every level, and I thought it would be good to mention those now.

Being Promoted "Over" Your Friends

This problem besets a great many of us. "Over" in this usage carries two meanings – getting the job when friends of yours also wanted it, and now, having to "boss" people who were once you peers. Every movement on the staircase carries with it these issues and problems with it. Many people compete for most promotions. We all know there will only be one appointment. Sometimes it is us; sometimes not. If it is not, wish the successfully chosen one the best, and offer to help. Even if you have to struggle to do this, it is the right thing to do. If you are the chosen, remember that everyone knew going in there was only going to be one winner, so do not feel guilty. Select those competitors whom you know best and with whom you have a personal relationship and go to with them for coffee. Indicate that you will continue to need their support, encouragement, and knowledge, and hope that they will continue to provide that (as you would have). Explore what kinds of things they were thinking about had they been selected, and offer to work with them to help make those improvements, although you may need to first get your feet wet. (This help suggestion may be more appropriate for a second meeting.) Remember, if they should feel ignored by you, those feelings will add fuel to the fire of their jealousy and envy. Indicate that you hope the personal relationship you have with them will continue.

In terms of personal relationships, these are now better carried on off site rather than at the office. And you need to be sure, if you do choose to socialize (and that is not a bad thing) in moderation that you do not have "buds" with whom you only or mainly socialize, ignoring the others.

In terms of supervision, it is often good to begin by asking what they think of as their assignments, duties and responsibilities, and the products for which they are responsible. Ask them to send you a memo ("I need to do this with everyone") and you can begin your work there. It is not easy, and you will adapt these suggestions to your own style and pace, but it is a start. And, it is much better than doing nothing and hoping for the best.

New Responsibilities at the New Level

New managerial supervisors, project managers, and middle managers often make the error of assuming the new job is just like the old job, only bigger. As such they tend to do *MORE* of what they did in the old job, rather then *SHED* those older duties and *EMBRACE* the newer ones. Perhaps shed is too strong a term, de-emphasize might be a better word. I am sure there is not a school principal in the world who, when a teacher, vowed **not** to be like the principal they had. And of course, when they became a principle, the inevitable happened. The chart in Figure 1 (Part 1, page 2) talked about the new duties you will need to assume, so keep that chart in mind. As you go through the next three chapters, keep in mind that in moving up, you add questions to be addressed and issues to be managed. Generally, things become more "integrational" (as in the orchestra conductor) and less performance based (as in the symphonic player). One of the things you need to shed as you move up is actually performing your old duties. Many a physician and clinician want to keep "seeing patients" as they move up the managerial ladder. It is not a good idea. Consulting occasionally, sure, but you need to refocus your time to managerial tasks. Just do it. Peter Synge (1990) talks about the "learning organization." What is also important is the "unlearning organization", being able to stop doing what you have done to make room available to start doing what you need to do. That insight is as true for people as it is for organizations.

The Total Compensation Solution

One of the courses I teach at the University of Michigan (this one at the Michigan Business School, but students from all departments at the University take it) is called "Reward Systems." It is sort of a "next generation" compensation and benefits course. In it, we look at what motivates people and how work "pays" for employee's commitment and performance. My research suggests similar conclusions to those of Coffman and Buckingham's (1999). While money matters, the "Softer Side of Sears" is dominant. It involves the opportunity to develop and grow, the need to do meaningful work in a place where one is appreciated, opportunity to have a quality life which includes work as a vital (but not total part), and the opportunity to have your unique needs met are vital to a thriving workplace.

ISSUES AND TECHNIQUES IN SUPERVISORY, PROJECT, AND MIDDLE MANAGEMENT

Introduction - Supervisory Management

In *Rules* the initial group of questions (boxed below) are called "base camp." These are the three things that managerial supervisors need to practice and deal with on a daily basis.

Base Camp - Managerial Supervisors [What Do I Get?]

1] Do I know what is expected of me at work?

2] Do I have the materials and equipment I need to do my work right?

3] At work, do I have the opportunity every day to do what I do best?

Three Major Foci

These issues are really the most important questions managerial supervisors need to answer for themselves, and for their supervisees.

1) Does the supervisee know what is expected?

This question not only refers to products, but also to accomplishments. Expectations revolve around work, presentation of self at work, willingness to help others, and so on. It would help if the supervisor had a little list of things that could be shared with the supervisee for example, "these are the things I expect" and/or "these are the things the agency expects". I mention both products and accomplishments because a good producer who erodes the accomplishment of others through "bad attitude" should be promptly dismissed . Bad attitude is contagious, and acts to quickly poison the work environment. If the employee does not know what is expected, then they cannot be fairly evaluated, so clarity is important for evaluative, as well as directional reasons.

2) Do I have the materials and equipment I need for my work?

Managerial supervisors need to develop a sense of what a worker needs to do the job. Materials and equipment may vary from setting to setting, but who among us has not subsidized our agency because something was needed and not available? Managerial supervisors may know what these materials and equipment are from their own experience, but should still keep an open ear and eye for more information about newer and better equipment and materials. And if employees do buy something on their own that is clearly necessary, be sure they get reimbursed for it, even if the amount is small. This is an issue of integrity for the organization.

3) At work, do I have the opportunity every day to do what I do best?

We all have tasks we are good at doing. Managerial supervisors should work toward the goal that every day each employee has some time to work on those tasks. Successful completion of what we do well, stokes our intrinsic motivation to do more. That said, it should not be read as doing only those tasks. However, there are a host of other tasks that organizations need to have accomplished, in which we should all take our turn. And there may be other parts of the job that we are not as good at but, we need to do anyway (for example, paperwork).

Conclusion

Managerial supervisors will be well served to use these three questions as the core of their work in managerial supervision. Answering just these questions is not, of course, enough. The answers are evolving, and so the discourse needs to evolve, and the specific applications crafted, and recrafted over time.

Introduction - Project Management

In *Rules* the next group of questions (on page 119) is called "mid camp." These are the four additional things that project managers need to practice and deal with on a daily basis.

+Mid Camp - Project Managers [What Do I Give?]

4] In the last seven days, have I received recognition or praise for doing good work?

5] Does my supervisor, or someone at work, seem to care about me as a person?

6] Is there someone at work who encourages my development?

7] At work, do my opinions seem to count?

Four Additional Foci

At least from my perspective, when one becomes a project manager, four more questions/tasks are added to the original portfolio. If the supervisor focuses on managing jobs, then the project manager, while continuing that oversight, is now working with bundles of jobs collected into projects. The same questions apply to the project as well as apply to the jobs, but, in addition, the project manager, because of the greater interconnectedness of effort projects require, needs to consider what might be called the person-at-work.

4) In the last seven days, have I received recognition or praise for doing good work?

Very few among us suffer from either over-appreciation or too much positive feedback. Recognition and affirmation are things that we all need to sustain us, especially when the "going gets tough." There are lots of ways to accomplish recognition, including thank you notes, sending flowers, a public e-mail, and the beat goes on. A book by Bob Nelson called *"1001 Ways to Reward Your Employees"* (1994) provides (you guessed it) a thousand and one suggestions about things one might want to consider doing.

5) Does my supervisor, or someone at work, seem to care about me as a person?

Each of us has "personal issues" that we are dealing with. These could span the range from trying to have a child to having a child, to the loss of a child, to issues with an elderly parent, to dealing with a child who is a drug user and living on the street, or whatever. While it is not appropriate for the project manager to get involved in these issues, it is appropriate to empathize, and to check in occasionally and see how things are going. If someone else is doing that, you can do it less. If no one seems to be attending to this matter, you need to do it more. All of us carry heavy burdens of a personal nature. They are ours to deal with, but an expression of interest is always appreciated. Appreciation and recognition sometimes means making accommodations (up to a point) to work schedules and flows. The other side of this is to help a worker recraft their job if they cannot continue to do the job they are in because of the personal issues they face.

6) Is there someone at work who encourages my development?

Part of caring about employees as people involves attending to their development and improvement – in a word, their growth. For me, the difference between this question and number 12 (This last year, have I had the opportunity to learn and grow?) lies in the difference between *this* job and the *next* job. Project managers work to help employees learn and improve at different facets of *this* job (different parts of the project).

7) At work, do my opinions seem to count?

We all know that those close to the job know how to improve the job. They may not know how their improvement may have other costs, but that is not up to them anyway. I once worked for an organization that had a shredder outside the meeting room in which we were gathering. Someone had stenciled on the shredder the words SUGGESTION BOX. The manager with whom I was working seemed totally oblivious to the message the stencil sent, and that its presence was a negative reinforcer. He thought it was cute. Part of accomplishment is helping things get better. This means that we like to make suggestions that help, and are pleased when they are accepted and get modest credit for them.

Of course project managers are attending to these questions/tasks with those they supervise, but they should also be helping managerial supervisors be alert to them with their own supervisees.

Conclusion

The project supervisor needs to build on the skills and foci of the initial level, and add an enhanced concern for the worker as a person, attending to her or his personal concerns in a modest but supportive way. Project managers need to help workers develop in the job they have.

Introduction: Middle Management

As one becomes a middle manager, a third set of concerns/skills emerges. Happily, they tend to refer to "work" as used in this book. Issues of mission (recall mission vs. margin) are a focus at this level. The sense (or not) that everyone on the same team (that is, within the whole organization), committed to doing quality work, and that whatever piece of the work pie they may own is also central. Development and growth are important too, but here, as I see it, the focus is on the career path rather than the task path.

+The Penultimate - Middle Mangers [Do I Belong Here? and Can We All Grow?]

8] Does the mission/purpose of my company make me feel my job is important?

9] Are my coworkers committed to doing quality work?

10] Do I have a best friend at work?

11] In the past six months, has someone at work talked to me about my progress?

12] This last year, have I had the opportunity to learn and grow?

Five Final Foci

8) Does the mission of my work make me feel important?

Meaningful work is of vital importance to workers. The interesting thing about meaningful work is that meaning is created by managers, rather than inherent in the work itself. Making meaning is one of the more important activities of the manager. It involves stressing the importance and ennobling elements of the work itself, and articulating the accomplishment that is achieved through completing that work. In 2002, National Public Radio (Speer) did a series on "dirty work" and who does it and why.
Here is there report on the Cincinnati Sewer System workers:

Aug. 29, 2002 –
Americans use roughly 450 billion gallons of water a day: 4.8 billion gallons just for flushing toilets, and the rest for bathing, washing or drinking. All that water eventually winds up in the sewers -- and that's where NPR's <u>Jack Speer</u> went, to meet the workers who keep the nation's waste flowing to treatment plants.

Speer and Morning Edition Associate Producer Melissa Gray visited Cincinnati's sewers as part of the show's series on "dirty work."

Americans' perception of sewer workers, Speer says, "is largely defined by one 1950s-era television show" -- The Honeymooners, in which comedians Jackie Gleason and Art Carney played bus driver Ralph Kramden and his pal Ed Norton, a sewer worker. Real-life sewer workers "aren't above joking about the work they do," says Speer -- but they contend their lives are nothing like a TV sit-com.

In hip waders, Speer and sewer worker Henry Chapman descend a 25-foot ladder into Cincinnati's aging sewer system. They walk into the mouth of a 20-foot-diameter pipe, part of what's known as a collection site that spews what Speer calls "an unsavory mix of storm water runoff and brown sewage."

These collection sites -- deep concrete containers where water flows through large grates -- are found throughout the 3,000 miles of pipe that carry waste to seven Cincinnati sewage treatment plants. And periodically, sewer workers say, the sites have to be cleared of sticks and debris that could keep the waste from flowing freely on to treatment. Jack Murray, whose job is to clean the grates at the end of the pipes, says over the years he's found some pretty interesting things there: "bicycles, tires, once in a while a door floating through..."

As distasteful as outsiders might find their jobs, Chapman, Murray and other Cincinnati sewer workers take satisfaction from the results of their cleanup efforts, Speer says. "Rather than doing a dirty job few people would want," he says, "they look at themselves as environmentalists improving the quality of peoples' lives."

Few people could imagine that wading through sewage in hip boots would have "meaning," but note the last paragraph. Meaning has been created.

9) Are my coworkers committed to doing quality work?

Few things are more irritating than being among the few committed to quality in an organization where lackluster performance passes for excellence. Middle managers need to set true standards of excellence, not "ok" standards. It is often argued that these standards are subjective and hard to articulate. Articulation is an important part of the job of the middle manager. Let me invite you to recall your teachers in grade school, high school, college, grad school, and beyond. By "beyond" I mean those community and family teachers who have/had a great impact on you. They could be a mom or dad, a grandparent, an uncle, an aunt, a sibling, or whomever. They had high standards, by high I do not mean rigid or meaningless ones. We all know, perhaps intuitively, that high standards and compliance standards are vastly different. We know the people who held us to our potential, who were tough, and who said rewrite, practice again, and one more time. For them we worked; for others we pretended to work. The best managers are like those teachers, family members, relatives, or community members. They expect the best and we are happy to give the best.

10) Do I have a best friend at work?

Managers cannot, of course, create best friendships with their supervisees. Perhaps best friend is a bit overstated, but most of us could have good friends at work. And, generally speaking, the workplace is the source of many of our friendships (neighborhood, church. synagogue, and school are others). Managers need to know, and be concerned about, the social fabric of the workplace. A socially connective and cohesive workplace is a creative and productive one.

Some of this concern takes the form of questions managers ask and awareness that managers develop. Are workers getting together in social situations? It can be in pairs, triads, or whatever. Activities can range from bowling leagues to dinner parties. But if there is not a substrate of social interaction in the organization, it is a jobplace, not a workplace. A jobplace is like a rest room – you enter, you do your business, and you leave. A workplace is where the jobs, tasks, and work intermingle to some extent and there is a feeling of camaraderie and community in the workplace. Of course, we compete there, but we also connect there. If there is no connection, no community, the workplace loses its psychic income; in the jobplace, that psychic income turns negative and the jobplace becomes toxic. Managers can create the conditions for friendships, and facilitate those that already exist.

11) In the last six months has someone at work talked with me about my progress?

12) This year, have I had the opportunity to learn and grow?

I have placed items 11 and 12 together because each focuses upon a similar theme – career pathing and growth. Everyone wants to learn and grow. The work I did in looking at compensation preferences in *"THE COMPENSATION SOLUTION"* (Tropman, 2001) suggests that "opportunity for growth" is one of the very important "soft" aspects of a workplace that employees desire. This desire has become important for four reasons. **First**, organizations are becoming flatter so there is less opportunity for advancement. Personal growth has replaced advancement in many cases. **Second**, increasingly in organizations, value comes from "headwork" and increased knowledge, gathered both in school and on the job, becomes important for the future. **Thirdly**, employees are less confident that they will remain in one place, so generalized knowledge, rather than localized knowledge, becomes key. The particular kind of growth many employees are seeking is the kind that is portable, rather than agency specific. And **fourth**, in part because of this expected agency mobility, employees are recognizing that they are responsible for their own career; the organization is not going to look after their interests at all.

This set of factors and concerns means that employees are looking for places where they can learn from managerial supervisors, projects managers, and middle managers. It means that teaching is one of the important components of the managerial world. While teaching goes on at each level, it is the middle manager who takes the most responsibility for this function. This assumption takes place in a number of ways.

One example is actual teaching. The best middle managers give seminars in areas of their expertise, and show up for sections of other ongoing training where their skills are relevant. They also walk the talk by attending, as students, trainings where they need to learn more. Few things are more impressive to employees than seeing their manager learn with them as a student in an appropriate area. Second, middle managers can and should encourage project managers and supervisory managers to add a teaching component to their supervision. Third, middle managers should work to assure that the agency incorporates teaching elements into its ongoing operations. This incorporation can include the support of in-service training programs, and through agency resources (time and tuition support) for personal educational goals. It also includes organization "harvesting" programs, where best practices from employees are reaped, organized, and made available to all.

But of course engaging in a buffet of activities does not assure that all employees are availing themselves of the opportunities. Hence, the career path discussion. That is where the question about progress comes into play. One cannot ask an employee about progress without reference to some planned journey. The career path is exactly that. Middle managers work to have all employees develop such a plan, which outlines where they want to go employment wise, what they need to get there, and by when. (It is, by the way, a great way to teach Gantt charting, because the employee's motivation skyrockets when the subject matter is herself of himself.) The plan may include stops within the current agency, but usually involves moving on at some point. Asking the employee how she or he is doing on their plan is one of the best ways to express sincere interest, and lots better than the parking lot question "Howzitgoin…gotta go!"

Conclusion

Middle managers, then work on the issues that managerial supervisors and project managers work on, but are especially responsible for meaning making, for connecting the mission of the agency to jobs, tasks, and work. The middle manager must ennoble the work of the agency, talk it "up" not "down, and convey its importance to all. Middle managers also insist on quality work at all levels, whether it is phone answering, or whatever task needs to have quality. Apart from the personal satisfaction that each of us gets when we do a quality job, it is vital to the agency because our consumer is a person in need, and vulnerable because of that need. They are not in a good position to insist on the quality they deserve. And then too, there is the famous phrase from the quality movement, "quality is free". That is because when quality is poor the agency needs to spend money on rework – fixing what was not done right the first time.

And finally middle managers need to attend to development, career pathing, and employee growth. Helping employees to learn supports them and gives the agency a more qualified worker. How cool is that?

Part **6**

CROSSCUTTING SKILLS

Introduction

There are some competencies that are crosscutting – that managers at each level need to know. Competencies involve knowledge plus skill. Their use will vary depending upon the particular set of assignments and agency situations, but they seem necessary always and everywhere. Dozens of focus group discussions and hundreds of individual discussions have confirmed these as central. I would not claim these are the *only* crosscutting skills. Other people may and surely will have other lists, but I do not think anyone will disagree, however, that these are central to effective management wherever management occurs, and at whatever level you work.

The words efficient and effective are in each competency. Efficient activities mean doing them the right way; effective activities mean doing the right ones. Doing things right; doing the right things. These are what is needed here. Efficiency is no good if you are going in the wrong direction; effectiveness is not any help if it takes too long. They are as follows:

1. Having Efficient and Effective Meetings
2. Making Efficient and Effective Decisions
3. Having Efficient and Effective Verbal Communication
4. Writing Efficiently and Effectively

The order here is based upon a "complaint gradient" that comes from the many managers and supervisors with whom I have worked. Meetings get the universal high score of "badness." Everyone seems to complain about them. The problems in meetings have become so common they are sort of like a national bad joke. Improvements in managerial meetings would yield big benefits in time saved

Meetings are called, of course, to facilitate decision making. While an army may move on its stomach, organizations move on the decisions the organization makes throughout its structure, from big ones to small ones. Building high quality decisions is an essential managerial accomplishment.

Meetings and decision making involve writing, and much of what a manager and supervisor does involves written communication. Becoming better at that skill, and understanding the range of documents that one routinely writes and how they can be improved, is important for any manager.

And finally there is verbal communication. Verbal communication is multifaceted that it involves what one says, how one says it, when one says it, what one does NOT say, and so on.

In each of these cases there is a huge amount of material available. Google lists 78 million hits for better meetings, 233 million hits for business decision making, 249 million hits for business writing, and 15.4 million hits for verbal communication. Obviously only a few tips and hints can be given here, but every journey begins with a first step!

Part 6 - Chapter **11**

PRODUCING EFFECTIVE MEETINGS

Introduction

Meetings are the hidden "cost center" of most organizations. The research I have done on meetings suggests that a massive amount of time is wasted in various kinds of useless meetings. And that is only the time *in* the meeting. When you add the time preparing for, going to, and returning from meetings, the costs in money, energy, and motivation are truly staggering. There seems to be broad agreement that meetings are deeply problematic.

Check out, for example, the cartoons on meetings in the New Yorker's Cartoon Bank (www.cartoonbank.com). The dozens of cartoons about meetings all represent the meeting of an inept gathering, a troubling social form. One liners, also confirm this broad assessment and take for example: "a camel is a horse assembled by a committee" or "a Board is a group that takes minutes to waste hours." In the meetings programs I put on for agencies, firms, and bureaus, I routinely use the title "Effective Meetings: How to get as little done as you do now in half the time." This joke phrase (which turns out to be approximately correct, actually) is always greeted by appreciative and knowing laughter.

Managers spend lots of time in meetings, whether they are one on one, in small groups, or in agency "events." We have every interest in having our time be well spent, and on the right topics.

Lessons From the Meeting Masters

Today you hear a lot about "evidenced based" practice and best practices. I talked earlier in this book about "harvesting" such practices. The material in this chapter and the next are "evidenced based" practices gleaned from my research on "meeting masters." "Meeting Masters" are several dozens individuals I have interviewed over the years who run meetings right. Some I discovered myself; in other cases masters suggested other masters to interview; sometimes colleagues, knowing of my interest, made the referral. It is what is called a rolling sample, or a snowball sample. The bottom line is that these women and men, from all kinds of organizations, pursued meetings in remarkably similar ways. When a person went into their meetings the difference from an "ordinary" meeting was palpable.

Five elements stood out:

1) the process was smooth and ran well (efficiency).
2) action happened.
3) decisions got made.
4) the decisions were of high quality (effectiveness).
5) the participants had fun.

Fun here means that they had an authentic experience, the meeting they were in was a **real** meeting (as opposed to the many fake meetings in which we participate). They provided accomplishment to the participants, something so rare in much of our worklife that we cherish the opportunity to participate in it when it is available. Everyone always attended the Master's meetings.

I have been able to distill their experience into a recipe, which I can share here and have shared at seminars around the world. It really works, but you have to actually do it. It is like diet and exercise: knowing what to do is an essential first step; doing it is the second step. The recipe consists of principles (general perspectives on meetings) and rules (the actual things you need to do).

The Principles

The Masters thought about meetings in different ways from most others. They thought of themselves as not "having" a meeting, but "producing" a meeting (as in a play) or "giving" a meeting (as in a party.)

A) The Orchestra Principle

Meetings work best if you run it like an orchestra. An orchestra performance represents the END of a process of development. The meeting should also represent the end of a process rather than the beginning. Orchestras have scores, which outlines what will be played, meetings should have agendas. Orchestras have the appropriate musicians present to play well and meetings should also have the appropriate players present including lawyers, teachers, and parents. Additionally members of the orchestra have been properly prepared prior to the performance. Key players in your meeting also should have been prepared in advance.

B) The Purpose Principle

There are three things that you do in good meetings: 1) you announce things, 2) you decide things, and 3) you brainstorm about things. Only the last two of these must be present to necessitate a meeting. Do not have a meeting unless you have a purpose – decision or brainstorming. If you do not have things to decide or brainstorm about, then do not have meeting. Many meetings are "newsletter" meetings ("here's what's going on in our organization") and could easily be canceled or condensed into a memo. Other kinds of meetings are "inform the boss" ("department X is doing this and department Y is doing that) meetings. The weekly meeting is often of this sort. These meetings should also be cut.

C) Three Characters Principle

Most meetings are driven by the "characters" (people) in attendance. The Masters organized the meeting by the character of the items. They began with a few announcements, then moved to the decision items, and then, at the end of the meeting, brainstormed about upcoming items to get some ideas onto the table. The thing to keep in mind is that decision-making involves an intellectual process, which goes from many to few and then to one. The brainstorming process involves going from one to a few to many. Therefore, it is better to do the same type of intellectual work at the same time and not go back in forth between the two. Decision-making must be done before brainstorming because decision-making breaks up group cohesion and causes people to become winners and losers. Brainstorming brings people back together and working towards the same goal. Brainstorming helps heal the emotional scars that decision-making leaves.

There is another reason to put brainstorming at the end. All meetings are divided into three parts. Meeting energy generally flows in thirds. The first third is called the "Get Go," which involves a few easy decision items and some announcements. The middle third is called the "Heavy Work" part and the last third is "Decompression." During compression (first third and second third of the meeting) people check out and drift away mentally. This is another reason why it is important to do brainstorming at this time because it re-engages people. Brainstorming allows people to switch gears and start thinking a new way, which helps bring them back in. Brainstorming is fun, non-threatening, and it gives people something new to focus on.

D) No More Reports / No New Business Principle

The Masters had no reports during their meetings. People who used to give reports are now asked to break up their material into announcements, decisions, and brainstorming items. This will allow your meeting to stay focused and not be derailed by new business. New business is, what you assigned to be worked on at the last meeting. The manager acts as the agenda scheduler and requests that meeting participants submit these items ahead of time. The supervisor can then put each item in its appropriate place and get any additional resources to deal with an item.

E) The Business Process Principle

Masters viewed meetings as a business process, the output of which is a decision stream. In that perspective, the process can be examined, considered, and improved.

The Rules

The rules are specific actions that the Masters took to create a smooth flowing process. An excellent process does not assure an excellent result, any more than good ingredients and a well equipped kitchen assures a good meal. But they are an excellent start to great results; without them, good results are often more random than realized.

A) The Rule of 1/2

The Masters got all the proposed agenda items 1/2 of the way between the meetings. That way they could compose the agenda, get both the information and people needed to be at the meeting in question, and get participants to think about what they needed from the meeting itself.

B) The Rule of 1/6

The Masters structured the agenda so that about 1/6 of the material was from the past, 4/6 from the here and now, and 1/6 from the future. They invited forward-thinking and creativity at every meeting.

C) The Rule of 3/4

At about 3/4 of the way between the meetings the Masters sent out the material. As one "meeting master" said, "giving people material at the meeting is like giving a musician a score and saying 'play this'; it is sight-reading and generally useless." The "deal" the Masters offered was this: I send the stuff out; you read it; we will get to it. They became like the professor for whom you always prepared.

D) The Agenda Bell Rule

The Agenda Bell (Figure 30) suggests that meetings begin with minutes, followed by announcements, some easy decision making items, then the harder decision making items, and then the most difficult decision items. The most difficult item is always located in the middle of the meeting where the greatest resources of attendance and energy are concentrated. If anything is going to break up the cohesion of the group it will be in the middle. Hence, brainstorming follows that and the meeting sort of winds (or more often, " whines") down to small trivial items like adjournment or items for an upcoming meeting. This style may take a while to get people into, but once they do, it can be self-reinforcing and enjoyable.

Tropman's Agenda Bell

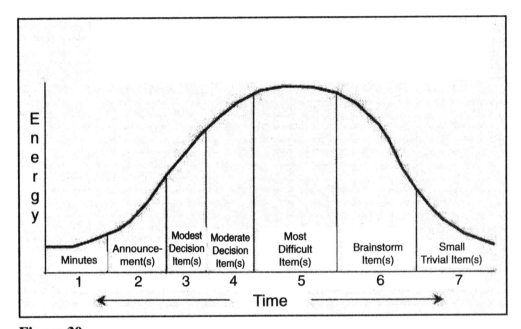

Figure 30

The Agenda Rule.

The best agendas are designed like a restaurant menu. Each decision is, like each dish, separately listed. Underneath each decision is a little phrase of explanation and the name of the person who is going to handle it. To the right is a running clock. Time units are used to signal the flow of the process. An agenda with no times is like a menu with no ingredients. (See Figure 31.)

An Agenda

Item#	Item Content	Time	Notes
1	Minutes	2-2:05	
2	Announcements – New Desks Ordered	2:05-2:10	
3	Retreat Location – Key West Seems Best – ACTION	2:10-2:15	
4a	Vendor Selection – A new Software Vendor Wishes to Make a Presentation ACTION	2:15-2:25	
4b	Medical Coverage Should we extend medical coverage to staff's gay or lesbian partners? ACTION	2:25-2:35	
5	Dress Code Should we retain casual Friday, go casual all week, or return to professional dress all week? ACTION	2:35-3:00	
6	Annual Community Appreciation Event Ideas for an exciting, different way to show our stakeholders that we appreciate their support BRAINSTORMING	3:00-3:38	
7	Adjournment	3:38-3:40	

Figure 31

E. The Rule of Minutes

Minutes are taken for substance, not court reporter style. Each item on the agenda has its own paragraph. The substance of the discussion is reported, usually in passive voice. (The mileage allowance was discussed. Some were in favor of x, others favored y, etc.) Then a line is skipped and the decision or action is placed in a box for easy reference:

> The group decided to review what other agencies are providing for their mileage. John will report back next week.

F. Rule of Paper

The Masters did not send out bulky packets. They sent out executive summaries, material that people will actually read. The plumper the packet, the less the participants will attend to it.

Conclusion

Much more detail is available in my book "Making Meetings Work" (2nd) (2002). This chapter provides a primer. Being a manager who runs great meetings will put you in a tiny class of esteemed executives whose expertise and presence is continually desired. It is sought because you produce a work process that is obviously better than anyone else. Enjoy!

Part 6 - Chapter **12**

BUILDING EFFECTIVE DECISIONS

Introduction

Having effective meetings that focus on decision making is not helpful if the decision making process is not understood and managed. Good decisions are the foundation stones of any organization. Unfortunately, all of us often make bad ones – individuals, groups, communities, organizations and societies. There is no sure-fire way to avoid bad decisions, but there are some techniques that can help us to make good ones. Decision making is a dynamic process, like the actual orchestra performance or the actual cooking of a meal. Once things are in "play" they are, well, in play. One needs to think on one's feet, go with the flow, go against the flow, know when to hold 'em and when to fold 'em. In short, Masters understood the deep structure of the decision making process – integrated both the intellectual and interpersonal elements, and managed both streams toward an intellectually robust and interpersonally acceptable solution. The likelihood of this happening without thought and attention is essentially nil. In fact, so common are rotten decisions that there is an entire selection of literature and jargon about them, including films. Let us begin on the dark side of decision making and look at some of the really awful examples common to all of us.

Rotten Decisions: A Banquet of Choice

We are all familiar with the "It seemed like a good idea at the time" phenomena in our agencies and our own lives. One current statistic is that about 1/2 of the people currently marrying become separated or divorced. That seems like bad decision making. And it *is*, up to a point. Decisions are designed to achieve results. For most decisions, if not all, the "result" or "outcome" is made up of the decision (the decision to marry, for example) and the implementation (making marriage work on a day-to-day basis). It is very possible, and we need to recognize this at the outset, that great decisions can be implemented in poor ways; it is also possible that poor decisions (you two are just not right for each other) can be made to work through creative and sustained attention to the issues of implementation. (Some of the people whom one thought should not have married did so, and have had a very successful relationship.) A little equation might be R =D+I (results equal decisions plus implementation). But we cannot rule out, also, the role of luck in outcome creation. Stuff happens – sometimes for the better and sometimes for the worse. Hence, a more complete equation might be $R = D + I +/-[L]$ (results equal decisions plus implementation plus or minus luck).

That said, we are talking about the decisions portion mostly, although, there is a bit of running together of course. Let's see what some classic bad decisions look like.

Folly

There are two versions of this idea. One version was developed by historian Barbara Tuchman, in her book *"The March of Folly"* (1984). For her, folly has to be: 1) a really bad decision; 2) picked from alternatives available at the time; or 3) made by a group, not an individual.

Steve Kerr talks about folly in his classic paper "On the Folly of Rewarding A While Hoping for B" (Kerr, 1995, p. 7-14). It is a situation in which one makes a decision for A and hopes it will result in B while actually focusing on A. This happens when people have a fascination with objective criterion, overemphasis on highly visible behaviors, particularly face time, hypocrisy (lying), and a failure to emphasize outcomes rather than outputs. Each of these should be familiar to supervisors as this is especially important to them. It is important for the supervisor to actually try to understand the work that employees do and get into the depth of that work rather than stay at the surface of "objective" criteria, overemphasis on visible behaviors ,and a constant reporting of activities rather than results. Many organizations reward output measures, rather than outcomes. For example, employees are "rewarded for face time" – being seen at the work site, rather than for the work they actually do.

Group Think

There are two versions of this type of decision-making (Janis, 1983). The first is the "don't break the peace" version, which is found in very cohesive teams. No one in these teams wants to provide bad news. The team members sort of agree with everyone else until something catastrophic happens to break up the team. The other version, known as "capitulate to power", applies when a powerful administrator makes a suggestion that everyone agrees with, but privately disagrees with. In this situation people often hesitate to speak up and voice concerns and issues because of the power dynamic. They may at a later time fail to support the decision, speak against it, or otherwise sabotage the decision process.

The Abilene Paradox

The Abilene Paradox is about the mismanagement of agreement (Harvey, 1988). It is a story about a family outside Abilene which drove into town for lunch, with no air conditioning in the car, in 120 degree heat, and as it turns out, no one actually wanted to go! It is the case where everyone does something that no one wants to do, but everyone thinks that everyone else wants to do it. What is vital here is that a decision be articulated so everyone actually knows that it IS a decision.

The Garbage Can Model of Organizational Choice

Michael Cohen, (with March and Olson) proposed this idea some years ago (1972). They make the point that all organizations have four kinds of people within them:

> 1) people who know the problems that are being faced by the organization;
> 2) people who can solve the problems that the organization faces, but may actually not know the problems because they are somewhere else;
> 3) people who control the allocation of money and other resources to a problem;
> 4) decision-makers who put it all together.

Cohen argues that most organizations assemble these people randomly as if tossed into a big hat. So, as you go through constructing a decision-making meeting agenda, ask yourself, "Do we have the people in this room who know the problems? Do we have people who can solve the problems? Do we have the relevant resource controllers? Do we have the relevant decision-makers?" If you are missing one of those groups, you will have to meet again. That is called rework and this method costs a lot of money.

The Boiled Frog

As I have mentioned earlier in this text, this is an old science experiment (Tichy & Devanna, 1986). If you put a frog into cold water and very slowly heat the water, the frog won't notice because it is a cold-blooded animal. The frog will eventually boil to death. If you put a frog in boiling water, it will jump right out. Change has this effect on us as well, it slowly works its way around us and it may not be noticeably different enough for us to take action. Suddenly we are dead. So we have to pay attention to when we act and act proactively rather than waiting for external pressures. The rate of change in your organization has to be slightly greater than the rate of change outside your organization or it will die.

Defensive Routine

A defensive routine occurs in an organization or a family for that matter, so this will be familiar to most supervisors and workers (Arygris, 1985). There is a topic within a group that is undiscussable. This is common for example, in families where substance abuse is an issue. "We will not discuss Dad's drinking." It goes deeper than that because the undiscussability is undiscussable. So we will not discuss why we are not discussing Dad's drinking. There are organizational topics that we will not discuss: differential rates of compensation, we will not discuss the fact that Sally is always coming in late, etc. And we won't discuss why we are not discussing those issues. These issues tend to fester until the organization faces some cataclysmic event and all heck breaks loose.

Managing the Decision

Decisions, like most things, go better if you follow well established practices rather than approaching them haphazardly. There are structured approaches to decision making that can be helpful. The leader needs to help the group with steps one at a time, in the same order and there must be a distinction between each step. Janis and Mann (1977) have a set of steps that are fairly well accepted:

- Need (What is the problem or issue? What do we need to do?)
- Alternatives (What are the alternatives available, or that could be available?)
- What does the evidence show?[1]
- Arguing about what the evidence proves.[1]
- Gains/Losses
    - self
    - others
- Pros/Cons
- Commit to Act
- Implement

[1]Janis and Mann did not have these approaches on their list; I added them.

As time goes on, groups will become familiar with this scenario and the benefits of following it. The group itself will enforce its application.

Decision Rules: The Deeper Structure of Decision Making

The step-by-step approach is enhanced if you have a bit more understanding of the dynamics of the decision process. This understanding involves some new concepts for you. These new concepts are as follows and each of these needs to be managed.

A.) Decision Rules,
   B.) Dominant Elements,
      C.) Decision Mosaic,
         D.) Rounds of Discussion,
            E.) Decision Crystallization,
               F.) Decision Sculpting.

A. Managing Decision Rules

There are rules to the decision making process that can help the process go better and increase the likelihood of a high quality decision. Decision rules are norms that make decisions "ok." The key element here is for managers to be aware that each of these "5" rules is at play in all decision making settings (even though some settings might privilege some over the others). A good definition of CONSENSUS is when an option meets, and can be shown to meet, each of these sets of interests. Managers must build a decision in a way that encompasses as many as possible. (See below decision crystallization.) There are five such rules. The reason they are usually used together is because each rule advantages a subset of the group and disadvantages others. Hence, the five provide a score of ongoing process of correction.

1) The Extensive Rule

The extensive rule takes into account what most people want. It is aimed toward creating the greatest number of participants and stakeholders. The drawback to this rule is that it always disadvantages the minority.

2) The Intensive Rule

The intensive rule counteracts drawbacks to the first rule by going with what makes people feel strongly, how strongly do they feel and can we accommodate them?

3) The Involvement Rule

The involvement rule gives power to the people who have to carry out the decision, what do they want, and how do they feel about it.

4) The Expert Rule

The expert rule takes into account what the experts have to say; this includes scientists, lawyers, and those with experience. Experts are not always right but we do not want to ignore them.

5) The Power Rule

The power rule is what the people in power or powerful stakeholders want.

These five perspectives are taken into account in order to build a decision that can meet and be shown to have met at lease the majority of the decision rules.

B. Managing the Dominant Elements

As with a puzzle, there are better and worse ways to start. With most puzzles you start with the corner pieces and the edge pieces. These might be called the dominant elements. Decisions have dominant elements as well. For example, consider a simple decision - "What shall we have for dinner tonight?" It is important to consider all the small parts of a decision then start the discussion with the dominant element. This is the element that will or most likely will affect all the other elements. Consider elements A through D.   Element A effects B, C and D; B effects C and D but not A, etc. If you should start with C, for some reason, then when you get around to A you will most likely need to rework C and D because of the effects of A and B. That is rework in the decision process, starting with A is what works best. There is no automatic way to identify A, however, so you have to think about the elements and come close, or as close as possible. In the evening dinner example, a good candidate is "in or out". It is a dominant element, which will affect all subsequent decisions, and indeed, in this case, the very decision path along which one travels. If the answer is "out", then you begin to think of places to eat. If the answer is "in" then you begin to think of what is in the fridge. This helps to avoid rework. (This is the Gettman Scale which I mentioned before.)

C. Managing the Mosaic

A decision element is the individual's piece of the mosaic. The word "decision" is really a collective noun. What we call a decision is most usually a bunch of small decisions put together. Decisions can be thought of as **built** or assembled, rather than "made". You "build" a menu made up of several decisions: peas or beans, chicken or fish, rice or pasta, chocolate cake or strawberry pie. It is a mosaic of elements that come together to form a decision mosaic. Understanding that decision making is a process of putting together a puzzle, is an essential perspective.

D. Manage Rounds of Discussion

A round of discussion occurs when everyone in a group has said one thing to contribute to the discussion. At that point, in almost every group, there will be a little pause or trough in the participation. That is a crucial moment in which a supervisor/meeting leader can intervene and speed up the meeting process. A supervisor should move the group to the next stage. If this does not happen, it is our natural tendency to continue talking about the same thing and delineate into unnecessary conversation. Discussions are like freeways, when you see your exit, you have to take it or else you will just go on and on.

E. Manage Decision Crystallization

Decision crystallization involves several steps. First, the supervisor summarizes what has been said during the round of discussion. They might use language like "what I heard was this, that and the other thing". This is a neutral summary, which organizes and presents back to the participants what they had been suggesting.

The next step, which flows right out of the summary, is a suggestion for action. This is called vocalization and presents an action to the group that it can take. But, presenting the action is not enough in and of itself. That action needs to be legitimized; the group has to be given reasons why it is okay. At this point we return to the decision rules to justify the reason that solution was presented.

Typically a decision manager will say something like this:

What I hear from the discussion is …. (you organize the main alternatives). It seems, therefore that a good possibility might be xxx (you vocalize a suggested action) because it would appeal to most people (extensive rule), it addresses the needs of the minority (intensive rule), it is ok with the ones who have to carry it out (involvement rule), the experts think it is ok (the expert rule, and the boss will sign off on it (the power rule.)

At that point, the group will ascent. This process can happen at random, but it works really well if you follow the protocol suggested here.

F. Decision Sculpting

After the mosaic has been assembled, piece by piece, you then step back to see what needs tweaking. You cannot see the whole thing from close up plus you also cannot see the whole decision early on in the process. Once you look at the whole thing, you can see what adjustments need to be made to make the whole decision better. For example, when you look at the entire menu for a meal, you can see that there might need to be an adjustment in some of the ingredients to make the overall meal more integrated. Similarly, as you look over all the elements of a decision mosaic, there may need to be some adjustments to the decision elements, which comprise it.

Overall, then, decision making is something that has parts and elements to it, you need to have a sense of the entire process as well as the specific. Managing the decision process is a key managerial task.

Conclusion

Decisions are the lifeblood of organizational jobs, tasks, and work. Everything we do depends upon decisions, big and small. It is odd, therefore, that managers do not think more about the decision making process, what is involved, and what practices and procedures would make it go better. Two sets of suggestions comprise the heart of this chapter. The first, the so called "rational decision making model," simply argues that if you proceed through an orderly set of steps, the outcomes will be improved. We would not argue that point in almost any venue, from cooking to golf, yet we seem not to attend to this in a decision making setting.

The second point is that there is a deeper structure to decision making than most people appreciate. It involves building decisions (the decision mosaic) from decision elements through rounds of discussion. At the end of each round (when everyone has said one thing or all those who want to say something have spoken once) decision crystallization occurs. This is a process through which the discussion is pulled together (summative reflection), followed by a suggested action (action idea), and then legitimized (using the five decision rules.) Legitimacy is required because there are conflicting norms (breadth of preference norms, depth of preference norms, involvement norms, expertise norms and power norms), which make decisions ok. These need to be harmonized as the decision crystallizer expresses the suggested action.

Part 6 - Chapter 13

WRITING EFFECTIVE MANAGERIAL DOCUMENTS

Introduction

Writing is one of the key ways that managers communicate. Much of the manager role involves writing, including preparing reports, memos, and to executives with other documents, as well as pulling together research information and technical perspectives. It is in the written document, most usually, that the manager's many lines of work come together (academic research, personal communication, policy and program history, and political information). In addition, the manager's own perspectives are also important.

The written word is important because it is "out there," has left the manager's hands, cannot be "taken back," and most of the time the interpretation of what is said occurs in the absence of the writer. In face to face communication you can ask me what I meant and I can explain. All kinds of questions need to be anticipated in the writing that managers do. Language matters.

But text is more than the form of the end product. Language structures the alternatives, facilitates or hinders consideration, and makes the processing of ideas easy or hard. Since policy is simply the writing of ideas, the language in which those ideas are expressed can make all the difference, especially if some of the ideas are new. Writing is also the way in which thought is organized and finalized. In this respect, the old saying "Writing is God's way of showing us how foolish our thinking really is" applies.

There are all kinds of documents that we write including memos, letters, reports, policy statements, and press releases. As with communication, there is a lot of material available, which you can access. And as in the last chapter on making effective presentations, there is no need to review all that material here. What I would like to do is share an "omnibus" system for organizing writing that I have developed, which I call the KnOWER System, and then make a few points that seem especially important to overall managerial writing generally. (See Tropman, 1984, for more detail.)

Reports: The KnOWER System[1]

Managers write all the time. The following Figure 32 touches on some key points and emphasizes one very important aspect of the writing process – there is rough carpentry and finish carpentry involved. Generally, writing works better if one begins with an outline – this allows you to play with the ideas (their sequence, order, and impact) in a sentence-free environment. Once you have that down, then you can fill in the text. The KnOWER system can help.

KnOWER stands for Knowledge, Organization, Write, Evaluate, and Rewrite. Each phase is part of the drafting process, and if the production of a draft can be viewed as a process, then the staffer can have some sense of the whole. For most purposes the KnOWER system provides a useful way to think through the issues and touch all the proper bases. As you become adept at such production, you will modify these rules and develop your own. This system is outlined in Figure 32, followed by a detailed discussion of each point. The discussion can only be illustrative, because too much detail is as harmful as too little. This discussion is aimed at providing a guideline that might have some use as a first step in managerial writing.

This recipe will obviously not work well if you apply it in a heavy handed fashion. You need to look over the template, and then adapt it as appropriate to your own portfolio of written work.

Let me say a little more about each area of the KnOWER System.

Knowledge (Kn)

Good writing begins when you have something to say, and an audience to say it to. (I know, I know; the word to, a preposition, is a bad word to end a sentence with!) Some work, therefore, in each of those areas is important. It really does not matter where you begin; finding out a little about your audience is crucial. Writing is, after all, marketing. It is important to know who will be getting the message.

After you get to know your audience, then take a look at what is already known about your topic. With today's ability to search for information on the web and through web based library sources, the ability to find out "what is hot and what is not" becomes crucial. Be sure, as well, to reflect, if not all sides, at least the important sides of crucial issues, where there is a division of opinion. One thing that people, who believe in something strongly, are often likely to do is to play up their side and ignore the other side. Take, for example, the issue of differences (or not) between male and female middle managers. There are opinions on the "differences" side and the "no differences" side. When the evidence is conflicting it is fine to draw you own conclusion from that evidence, if two conditions are met. One condition is that you present the two or more sides. The second is that you explain the basis or bases on which you made your choice. "My own experience suggests" is a fine basis, as long as you articulate it. Also, be sure and keep a record of your sources. You may need them later and others may ask for them. If you say "Research shows…" you better have that research handy!

The KnOWER System for Managerial Writing

Knowledge (Kn)
   I. Define the Problem – know the audience
  II. Secure Information About Problem
       a. Academic information
            i. the library
           ii. computerized data banks
          iii. reports, fugitive documents, available from agencies
           iv. use the phone to secure information from around the community and country
            v. personal informants
       b. Political information
            i. talk to key individuals
                 1. elites
                 2. people-in-the-street
           ii. touch base with key groups
          iii. check any formal requirements
       c. Historical information
 III. Redefine the Problem

Organization (O)
   I. Make an Outline
  II. Place Summary First
       a. Problem
       b. Options
       c. Your recommendations
       d. a-d generally come in the first paragraph of a letter or memo, or the first pages (executive summary) of a report
 III. Text repeats and elaborates on the key parts
       a. Problem
       b. Findings
       c. Options
       d. Recommendations
  IV. Appendix

Write (W)
   I. The Draft Idea
       a. Write drunk; revise sober
       b. Get ideas onto paper quickly
  II. Political Language
       a. Watch pronouns, etc.
 III. Writing Hints
       a. Quick period – use short sentences
       b. Vary language
       c. Anchor with illustration
       d. Write to press release - that is (as in III. a. above, write as if readers will only look at the initial material)

Evaluate (E)
Rewrite (R)

Figure 32

Organize (O)

Organization is the rough carpentry of writing. It is, essentially, the outline. It is a really great idea to outline first, because you can more easily see the flow of the argument and the steps through which you want to take the reader, without too many words. It is sort of like what my grade school art teacher said, "When you draw a tree start without the leaves. That way the structure of the branches is clear. After you get that framed, then you can add leaves." Words are like leaves. The outline need not be detailed, though it can be, but the main points need to be there. Organize the evidence, then go to the next step.

Write (W)

Once you have the outline down, add words to each part. It is much easier to write once you are following an outline. As I mentioned, get stuff down quickly. Do not self-censor yourself; that comes in the next step. You do not have anything to look at if you do not have anything on the page! For short writings set yourself a time goal – say 1 hour for a letter, or memo. For longer documents set yourself a page/time schedule – 3 pages a day, or whatever. By the end of the week you will have a draft of 15 pages.

Evaluate (E)

Evaluation is a two part process. The first part is looking it over yourself and making changes. But it is essential, in my view, to wait at least 24 hours before you look at the draft again. There needs to be some time between the current draft and your revisiting it. It is sort of like rebooting your computer. You have to wait a couple minutes so the memory can clear out.

The second part of the review is getting reactions from others. This is both an intellectual and a political process. On the intellectual side, you want to give copies (not of every document but of important documents) to those whom you believe can evaluate the strength of your argument and presentation and give constructive feedback. Remember that it is not necessary to follow every suggestion, but it is good to get a variety of perspectives. It is also important never to argue with or dissent from this kind of feedback. Ask them for it; accept it as feedback, not as something you will necessarily do. If you argue with responders, they will back away from responding (the asker is too high maintenance) and simply tell you it is great. Thus the value of feedback is lost.

Politically you sometimes want to show your material to "important" people or "opinion leaders." It is vital to know what parts may be politically sensitive and what words might be seen as outrageous.

In each case, be sure to thank your reviewers at the time they give you the feedback and in the document (though not in simple letters and memos). Sometimes you can work their comments and suggestions in as quotes or personal communications. Your draft is strengthened if you use the words and authority of others as well as your own. Microsoft Word now has a track changes feature, which allows suggestions to a text to be followed easily. Make use of it if you can.

Rewrite (R)

After you have read the suggested changes, spend some time thinking about what you want to include and what not. Then prepare a second draft. Important documents often go through three plus drafts, so be sure and plan your time accordingly; otherwise, plan on working late.

Conclusion

The KnOWER system (Knowledge, Organization, Write, Evaluate, and Rewrite) is designed to help managers be more effective in their writings and in communicating the ideas they wish to convey. Keep in mind that the goal of writing "well" is not a literary one. Rather, it is an attempt to convey ideas, to develop these ideas, and communicate them in the managerial process.

---

[1]The original, and much longer, version of the KnOWER system appears in J. Tropman. Policy Management and the Human Services (New York: Columbia University Press, 1984)

Part 6 - Chapter 14

CREATING EFFECTIVE
MANAGERIAL COMMUNICATION

Introduction

One of the skills that all managers need (from bottom to the top) is effective verbal communication. People with whom you work need to understand what it is you are saying, and what you mean by what you say. There is an old story (called the Three Penguins Story) that illustrates the problems that can occur when communication goes awry.

The Three Penguins

A man is driving down the road and he sees three penguins along the roadside. He stops, picks them up, and puts them into his car. As he pulls in to get some gas, the attendant says "You have three penguins in your car; You should take them to the zoo." "You are so right" says the driver, and off he goes.

About a week later the gas station attendant is out and notices the same car from a week ago he had seen with the same penguins. He looks into the car and, sure enough, there are three penguins in the back seat; except this time they are wearing sunglasses.

"Aren't you the guy I saw last week" asks the attendant?
I am, " says the driver. The attendant says "I thought you were going to take those penguins to the Zoo." "I did, the driver replies. We had a great time. This week we are going to the beach!"

Little can illustrate the perils of communication in management better than this story. The more important question, perhaps, is how to get it right, or at least better.

For purposes of managerial communication, I want to emphasize three key areas, with the understanding that there is so much more out there and communication is the subject matter of entire books, magazines, and academic departments. These are 1) **Intrapersonal**, 2) **Interpersonal**, and 3) **Transpersonal** (phoning and speaking). My selection is again based upon talking with and observing managers over the years and coming to understand that there are a few simple things that we can all do to improve our communication.

Begin with the Audience

At least one common theme runs throughout each of these kinds of communication and it is useful to introduce that here. It is the audience. All communication has an audience, whether the person you are communicating with is yourself, others, or a larger group. All communication begins with the target – what is it that you want that audience to comprehend? In social work we have a phrase, "start where the client is", which applies exceptionally well to communication. Start with the audience, is a really good rule to apply on a daily basis. It is useful to repeat Steven Covey's injunction "Seek first to understand, then be understood" (Covey, 1990). One might think Covey has it backwards, because the key element in managerial communication is to be understood. But Covey realizes that if one does not understand the audience and where that audience is coming from, then communication cannot be tailored to be effective.

1) Intrapersonal

Intrapersonal conversations are conversations you have with yourself. You may not have thought that the person you talk most with is probably you. This internal language and dialogue can contain negative self-talk and negative constructs. Negative self-talk usually sounds like, 'I can't' or 'I'm dumb'. These thoughts can impact our interaction with others and erode a manager's ability to provide support to those they supervise. Negative constructs can be something like 'the problem, system, task, etc… is dumb'. We have seen negative constructs pretty frequently when we watch our kids trying to tie their shoes.

> An example might be the two Moms who are watching their kids try to tie their shoes. One kid is not getting it, and is crying in frustration. The other Mom asks "Why don't you help him?" The crying kid's Mom replies, "I am helping him."

When they cannot do it, they say, 'this shoe is dumb' because they are frustrated. There is a little bit of that kid still in all of us and we have to watch for those problems to emerge. These internal conversations can inhibit organizational change, as individuals complain or blame rather than constructively plan.

We also need to silence our inner critic. Negative self-talk can initiate and support negative circularity and a downward spiral or self esteem (Hein, 2004, p.188). Instead of giving into these negative internal thoughts, managers can and should work on positive reflections and savor our strengths. We need to do this regularly because in a high-pressure job, it seems sometimes our problems are greater than our strengths.

Much of our internal conversation involves reinforcing our assumptions. We think we "hold" assumptions, but, often in reality, it is our own assumptions that "hold" us. When we think of ourselves as choosing the assumptions we hold, we can also then recognize the possibility of changing those assumptions. This is one of the key points in the work of Robert Kegan and Lisa Lahey in their book "How the Way We Talk Can Change the Way We Work" (2001). That's the danger of bad assumptions and that is why we need to scrutinize them carefully. Supervisors' assumptions about workers and their work need constant reexamination and reflection. Charles Horton Cooley, a famous University of Michigan sociologist said, "Things thought to be real are often real in their consequences."

2) Interpersonal

Managers also need skills in interpersonal communication. There are several aspects of this understanding that are important and they are as follows:

A) Communication Style

Managers need to understand their own style of communication and its implications. Very much like the idea of temperament (the Myers Briggs Assay is a temperament assay) there are many assays of communications styles available. Again, as in temperament, it is useful to have a read on these without taking them to be completely defining of yourself.

One very good available book is *"STRAIGHT TALK: Turning Communication Upside Down for Strategic Results at Work"* (1998) by Eric Douglas. Douglas suggests that there are four basic styles as outlined below. He also argues that we tend to use two of them more than the other two. The four styles are called: (1) Director, (2) Thinker, (3) Expresser, and (4) Harmonizer. (See Figure 33.)

Four Basic Styles of Communication from Douglas

(1) DIRECTOR	**(3) EXPRESSER**
Talks in action verbs	Speaks rapidly
Cares about the "bottom line"	Uses animated gestures
Always on the go	Entertaining
Speaks crisply	Thinks out loud
Talks about goals	Talks about ideas
May seem insensitive	May be imprecise
(2) THINKER	**(4) HARMONIZER**
Talks about details	Talks about people
Inquiring	Sensitive to others
Often makes lists	Avoids conflict
Speaks carefully	Dedicated and loyal
Wants things done "right"	Speaks softly
May procrastinate	May over commit

Figure 33

It would be useful for the manager to develop a fuller understanding of their own style, and as well, the order of preference of styles they have. If Douglas is right, two of these will immediately seem "right" to you. The other two will seem less close and comfortable. When you have completed the self-analysis, then you should seek to understand the styles of others. When you start with the audience in mind, seek to appeal to them not as much through **your** style, although there will always be some of that, but through **their** style.

B) Gender and Communication Style

In her book, "You Just Don't Understand," Deborah Tannen (2001), talks about the communication styles of women and men. Again, it is helpful to remember that not all women and not all men follow gender-unique communications styles, but her points are useful to keep in mind. In particular, she suggests that the fundamental purposes of communication may be different. Men, she suggests, engage in "report talk" which involves directing, conveying information, the use of overheads, newsprint, etc. to emphasize our points. Making a connection with the audience is secondary. Women, on the other hand, engage in "rapport talk," the primary purpose of which is to establish connection, with the conveyance of information as second. It is a very interesting idea, and one which we should all keep in mind as we go about our daily work.

C) Avoiding Communication Traps

Managerial communication, especially with subordinates and peers, can entrap the manager in surprising ways. One of these ways is called the "monkey-on-my-back" phenomenon. It occurs when the subordinate comes in and complains about something that they cannot do. The manager, especially in the helping professions, is likely to try to be helpful by assisting in the task, and sometimes taking over the entire task! A better approach is to train your staff in "creative complaining." "Creative complaining" means that anytime someone comes to you with a problem they also have to have at least one solution to the problem. The conversation starts with the solution, not with the problem.

D) Blame and Credit

Significant parts of managerial conversations involve giving credit and assigning blame. A concept called "the mirror and the window" is useful to remember here. As humans, we have a tendency to look in the mirror when credit is to be assigned and out the window when blame and responsibility is to be distributed. The opposite is a better practice. When problems arise it is better to look into the mirror rather than out the window. Looking in the mirror requires first assessing our own contribution to the problematic situation and then looking out the window at the contribution of others. It is good to remember that for every finger of blame pointed at someone else, three fingers are pointed back at you.

E) Praise in Public, Blame in Private

Continuing on with the theme of credit and blame, the setting makes a huge difference. It is important to give praise in public. Praise gives employees the encouragement to continue with their work and also lets them know they are doing the job correctly. Managerial supervisors who practice praising regularly know that they get more leverage from a good comment if others can hear it, as well as the specific intended recipient. Criticism is always done in private, to avoid shaming employees in front of peers or other supervisors. It also avoids people feeling as though they must defend themselves to the group. One would think such an obvious point need not be made, but there is a significant number of managers who feel that public humiliation is a good motivator (it is, but motivates only hate and sabotage) often, manages to avoid praising in public because they feel it detracts from them.

F) Coaching and Counseling

Whetten and Cameron, in their book "Developing Management Skills" (6th) (2005), have an entire chapter on managerial communication. One point they make is exceptionally interesting for purposes here – the difference between Coaching Communication and Counseling Communication.

Coaching is the informational work of supervision. Managerial supervisors coach when they pass along information, give advice, set standards of performance, and/or help staff to improve. Problems with coaching arise when a supervisor does not have all the information, does not fully understand the nature of the problem, or is not letting the worker practice the coaching suggestions (coaching incorrectly). Supervisor's responses during these times are direct. They must advise, reorganize and provide suggestions.

Counseling is the emotional work of supervision. Managerial supervisors must counsel when an employee's attitude is interfering with the task at hand. In these interactions, the employee may appear defensive and project their difficulties on others. They also may have difficulty recognizing the nature of the problem and may not be show much willingness to change. Counseling problems stem from fear of fault, blame, failure, and success. Some problems can however be simply attributed to temperament clashes. Counseling responses are non-directive. The supervisor must probe for information, reflect upon what the employee communicates, validate the employee's affect, and ask for answers. Asking for answers means that the employee needs to come equipped with some solutions to the problem they are bringing to the boss for consideration.

G) Feedback

We all need and like both positive and negative feedback about our work. Positive feedback helps us to know that we are moving in the right direction. Negative feedback can give guidance about places for improvement. Despite this, some employees may experience a fear of feedback. Part of this fear may not come so much from the feedback itself but from the clumsy way that it is delivered. If feedback is not handled in an appropriate manner, valuable information is lost. The danger lies in managerial supervisors who give feedback in such a bad way that employees do not listen to it and focus only on the emotions evoked by the information. This can lead to one party blaming the other.

Effectively given, feedback probably is THE best performance improver. Managerial supervisors need to understand that feedback is different from criticism and should be focused on the problem rather than the person. Feedback is non-judgmental and non-fateful observation about how anyone (subordinates, peers, or bosses) can improve their performance. Feedback should be problem oriented, connected to the topic, and close in time to the event. The person providing the feedback should be able to accept their part of the problematic situation. It should be descriptive and validating. Managerial supervisors should avoid criticizing or evaluating the employee in the feedback context. Managerial supervisors must also "own" their feedback and not make the source an unknown or someone else. An example of "non-ownership" might be "I wanted to give you a raise but "they" (Human Resources, Top Management) would not let me. This is a lie.

Managerial supervisors should allow the feedback to be a two-way conversation and avoid lecturing. Managerial supervisors should share information that is focused on behavior. They should also focus on the needs of the receiver and the feedback should be directed towards something the receiver can change. It is also best if the employee solicits the feedback, but this is not always possible. Managerial supervisors should avoid giving direct advice and use phrases like, "Perhaps, … Something which has worked in similar situations…,You might consider … etc that allow the employee to "choose" the suggestions, rather than being ordered to do it.

Another way to open a conversation in which you intend to give feedback is to start by asking the employee about their motives and thus, will help you better understand the problem. Always check for comprehension prior to ending the conversation. Feedback cannot be done once a year, it needs to be done often and as timely as possible.

Feedback conversations need to be distinguished from those of a "disciplinary" nature. When outcomes and outputs have not been met, then consequences follow.

3) Transpersonal Communication

Some kinds of communication are what I call transpersonal – meaning there are people involved but not exactly face-to-face. Two examples are use of the telephone and the making of presentations.

The Telephone

Telephone communication is something managers often overlook because it is so common and ubiquitous. Yet it is a verbal communication and needs to be considered.

The same principles of good communication generally apply to the phone, except that we tend not to think about it that way. The phone is, well, the phone. But remember that tone of voice, sense of friendliness, appropriate pace and cadence, are very important. If you have trouble getting people on the phone, and getting people to call you back, it may be because they recognize that you are one who speaks slowly, who uses circumlocutions, who is a seeker of help, rather than a giver of help. In short, you are and will always be a "high maintenance" caller. Naturally, folks would not want to answer the phone or call you back, let alone call you in the first place!

There are many excellent websites that can provide information on telepone comunication skills. I have summarized a few key points on the next page under Telephone Skills.

Telephone Skills

1. **Preparing for the Call.**
   A call is like a meeting. Make some preparations both in writing and emotionally, if necessary. If the call is complex, their fax or e-mail an agenda to your talking partner(s).

2. **Establish Time Parameters**
   It is important to let calling partners know how long you will be available. You need to schedule the items so that you can complete them over the available time. Begin with easy items, place the tough ones in the middle, and end with brainstorming, as suggested in the chapter on Efficient and Effective Meetings and the Agenda Bell.

3. **Ending the Call**
   Very much like leaving a party, some calling partners will linger and linger. It is important, therefore, to alert folk's partners when there is about 5 minutes left for you. If necessary, use some of that time to schedule another call.

4. **Follow Up Promptly**
   Once the call is complete, make notes and send them to the calling partners with appropriate follow-up information.

5. **Angry Calls - When You are Angry**
   Many of us pick up the phone and call when we are angry. This is not a good idea. We are less clear and cogent when we are angry, and our anger brings out defensive anger in others. A better plan is to send a note sharing your thoughts and feelings, and follow up with a call that can focus on the elements in the note.

6. **Angry Calls - When Others are Angry**
   As a recipient of an angry call, try not to enter "the dance of anger." Simply accept what the caller is saying, as information, not agreement. It is often ok to apologize... even if something is not your fault, you can apologize for an unfortunate occurrence.

The Presentation / Speech / Remarks

Presentations involve speaking to groups of people. One is tempted to say "rather than interacting with them" but that would be wrong, since you are interacting with them, but not exactly in the same way as in a meeting or discussion group. Google "presentations" and lots of material is available to you. This is not the place to summarize a lot of available material on how to make your presentations more effective. What I am going to do instead is present a number of important tips on making presentations. I invite you to integrate these with your own experience and with available written material that speaks to your style:

Tips on Making Presentations

a. Watch the clock.—Far and away, presenters say too much and talk too long. Less is more. Practice your timing, as many people do not have a good sense of how long their presentation actually take.

b. Speak from an outline—an actual text "begs" you to read it, and as you look up from a text it is hard to relocate yourself in your text so you look like a fumbler.

c. Prepare your text in larger 14 of 16 point font; as it is much easier to follow.

d. Make Copies Available—Provide copies for the audience to follow. Include your name and contact information there so people can follow up.

e. Use PPT—Power Point is great - it helps you brief up your remarks, and provides visuals as well. Do not hesitate to include photos and other "eye candy" to make your work attractive.

f. Appropriate humor—If you tell a joke or story, be sure it relates to the point you are making.

g. Create Participation—Whenever possible, invite people in groups or at tables to have a discussion about your material and then invite some to share the results for all to hear.

h. Game films—Watch and listen to how you present. It may be painful, but you may get a good sense of some negative mannerisms you did not know you employed.

Conclusion

Communication is a process (a developing process) of achieving mutual understanding. Understanding does not mean, nor does it require, agreement. That is a separate process. One cannot negotiate from the basis of a flawed understanding of the issues at hand. Begin by understanding the audience. Try to get a feel for the group or person to whom the message is directed. Then consider the communication you have with yourself. You are your toughest and most constant critic. Try to get some idea of your preferred styles of communication – and the conditions under which they are likely to be poor first choices! Consider also the role that gender (and other social categories) might play into your style. And always remember Covey's dictum, "Seek first to understand, then be understood" (Covey, 1990)

Part 7

ORCHESTRATING MANAGERIAL CHANGE

Introduction

I have already introduced the topic of managerial change in Part Three and talked about changes in foci. Part Four, similarly, dealt with undercurrents of change. And in Part Five, I talked about the learning curve, and the unlearning curve, and the unpacking and repacking of competency bundles, is centrally related to change. Each of these three areas, though, follows a similar path – from novice to beginner to journey person to expert to master. Managers need to know where they are on the "Managerial Staircase" and how to both relate to others on different steps and to help others (and themselves) keep progressing. This will be discussed in detail in Chapter 15.

A second issue of importance to consider is the pitfalls and land mines that lie in the path of the manager as they move from managerial supervisor to project manager to middle manager and beyond. The "beyond part" focuses on the Executive Leader - CEO/President/Chief Professional Officer/ Executive Director. I will not be dealing with those positions and roles in this volume, but will do so in the next volume – Executive Leadership in the Human Services. But there is danger of derailment and of the patterns of behavior that lead up to derailment.

These are the dangers that all managers face. And if derailment and periderailment get in the way of success, then what is success? This is the classic American question. Some say money; some say power; some say prestige; some say the "perfect job." But it seems, whichever one we pick, the others lure us. In this concluding chapter of the book I look at the need to define and manage our own success.

A CIRCULAR STAIRCASE OF MANAGERIAL COMPETENCE

Flow: The Psychology of Peak Performance

Introduction

For workers to be performing at their best, they must be at the intersection of challenge and skill. This is called being "in the flow." If workers are not challenged, they can become bored. If they are challenged too much beyond their current skill, they become anxious. Workers who fall in either of these states (boredom or anxiety) are prone to worker failure. The role of the supervisor is to understand where the worker is and which tasks are appropriate for that worker. It is also important for the supervisor to help challenge a worker to move up in skill level by adding appropriate increases in task level.

This is particularly important in child welfare settings, where employee turnover is frequent. Also the pressure of the child welfare setting can push managerial supervisors to expect more from new employees, based on their skill level, than they should. We also recognize that child welfare workers may turn over quickly to attain higher levels of performance—either by leaving the agency or by lateral transfer. The Flow Chart (Figure 34) demonstrates this relationship between worker challenges and skills and the effect of this relationship on caseworker behavior. The flow channel shows the balance between worker task and skill is more than the managerial supervisor should expect. Once this balance is reached, it must be maintained by increasing task complexity as skill levels increase.

The Flow Chart of Competence by Csikszentmihalyi (1990. p.78)

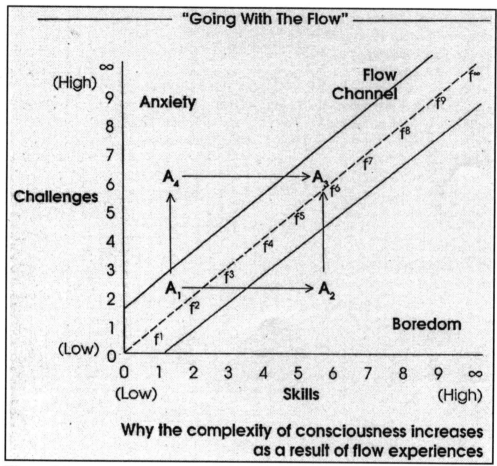

Figure 34

From Novice to Master

As you look over flow chart Figure 34, you can see that at the bottom (1,1) we have a simple task, requiring simple skills. The person here is a novice, whether he or she is a child welfare worker, cook, learning a new language, or learning to ride a bike. Over time we should all move up the flow channel, aiming for a 9, 9 and beyond as this is the master level. In between the novice and master levels are levels of beginner, journey person, and expert. This chapter will detail the skill levels of each and then outline the ways in which managerial supervisors can assist in their employees' skill progression, based on the work of Hubert & Stuart Dreyfus in "Mind Over Machine" (1986).

Novice

Novice workers often perform tasks in a slow and uneven manner. They tend to pay close attention to rules and facts. This is the stage when an employee does many things by the book. During this phase, employees learn the most about procedure and rules. This is important in child welfare work due to the many federal and state mandates that dictate practice implications. The problem during this phase is that a worker does not gain much reinforcement from the tasks they perform. They may not find the task itself to be gratifying or rewarding because they may still not be meeting standards (even if and when they are doing the best they can), simply because they are new to the work. Additionally they may be receiving only negative feedback and very little reinforcement. The only satisfaction employees may feel at this stage is from completing the task, not from doing it well. During this stage, novices require additional training from their supervisor.

Beginner

At this stage an employee's performance becomes faster and smoother. They begin to discover patterns not mentioned in the rules. These employees do not use the book as often and they begin "rule fade." Employees are still learning at this stage. Problems arise at this stage due to embarrassment. Employees are just beginning to understand what is required of them and what might have episodic pitfalls. These pitfalls may be instances where they use the wrong language or the wrong skill in an incorrect place. These instances tend to be episodic and so the employee is never quite sure when they might occur. This can result in anxiety and embarrassing moments for employees. During this stage, employees require additional coaching from their supervisor.

Journey Person

A journey person's performance is notable for its speed and smoothness. At this level, rule fade is almost complete. Journey persons will select only the most important cues (the cues will be the important/relevant information coming in) and ignore "noise." A cue is a vital piece of information about an ongoing process. For cooking, it might be the sound of the frying pan, or the smell; for music it might be a certain note. For child welfare it might be certain behaviors (killing pets, for example) or whatever. Additionally they are now taking calculated and educated risks. They consult the manual only on exceptions. Even though they are still learning, they may have also begun to teach those around them. At this stage, they still require the supervisor to teach and share information with them. The problem at this stage can be that the journey person thinks it is the end of their learning process and may be resistant to information from managerial supervisors. Employees at this stage require additional teaching from their managerial supervisors.

Expert

When an employee reaches the expert stage, the need to calculate and rationalize diminishes in their decision-making process. Decision-making tools such as structured decision-making become an integral part of their conceptual framework. Their performance becomes fluid, quick, and sure. Their attention shifts as cues (important case information, for example) shift. They have a holistic and intuitive grasp of the work. They no longer consult the book and think they could write the book. Experts take on a much greater teaching role at this time. The challenge of the supervisor is to except this improvement from the worker. The supervisor and expert now must mutually explore problems to create fixes in the system. At this skill level, some experts can fall prey to "expert lock." This is when employees tend to do what they are best at and may inappropriately generalize their expertise to everything else. They may need education from a supervisor to recognize their own limitation.

Master

Once the skill of master is reached, a worker's performance is seamless. It is solid, confident, and sure. Their work is done at exactly the right speed and it appears effortless. Masters understand the deep structure of effort. They have a holistic recognition of cues. They deeply understand and see beyond the obvious. Masters trust themselves and the process. They are able to let the process flow and enter when needed, working beyond the book. At this skill level, employees need a mentor to help them in their career development. Managerial supervisors are also able to use this worker as a teacher for others. The problem employees may encounter at this level, may involve their ability to access their knowledge and self. People who make it to this skill level tend to be in high demand and managerial supervisors must protect these employees from both formal and informal extra workloads. At this stage employees need mentoring.

The Role of the Supervisor in an Employee's Move from a Novice to a Master

The Novice: Training (90/10)

When a supervisor begins with a novice, his or her initial role is to make sure the employee understands what is required of them as well as workload requirements. The supervisor should spend time reviewing these things with the employee. Narrow the policy/practice gap for employees by giving them simplified and sequential instructions on completing tasks. Managerial supervisors should give a small number of cases to new employees. Managerial supervisors should be reviewing 90% of an employee's work at this stage (90/10). Training is often done in groups for new employees or when new requirements need to be disseminated. Training in child welfare can occur in both the field or an outside educational setting.

The Beginner: Coaching (70/30)

When working with employees who are at the beginner skill level, it is important to be assured that they understand the job requirements. Because child welfare work is based upon a policy/practice manual, the job of the supervisor is often to interpret manual policy and disseminate it to employees. Managerial supervisors at this stage serve to provide tips and suggestions. They pass along information, apply standards from manual, and advise workers. By providing staff with adequate information, you can help them to better their performance. Here managerial supervisors should review 70% of an employee's work (70/30).

Journey Person: Teaching (60/40)

Employees who need teaching are in the journey person stage. They need help mastering and improving requirements and routines. Managerial supervisors should review 60% of an employee's work (60/40) at this level. The employee should review manual policies on his or her own and select work products to be reviewed by the managerial supervisors.

The Expert: Educating (40/60)

Experts are concerned with improving practice routines and requirement as much as possible. Managerial supervisors can assist in this process and also answer questions from the employee. Experts will bring best practice from elsewhere. Managerial supervisors should be reviewing 40% of an employee's work (40/60). An employee at this level knows enough to improve requirements formally and informally.

The Master: Mentoring (10/90)

While mentoring, it is important to keep in mind that employee growth is the focus of the interaction. At this level, both employee and supervisor should be looking to the future. Mentoring begins when you go beyond your job responsibilities in a voluntary, caring, sharing, and helping relationship. A supervisor should prepare to work with his or her mentees across the whole mentoring spectrum, from participating in employer sponsored formal programs, to creating interpersonal informal relationships. A supervisor should mentor all associates according to their special needs. Managerial supervisors should only be reviewing 10% of an employee's work (10/90) at this stage.

Figure 35 recaps the skill levels and managerial needs associated with each level, from novice to master.

From Novice to Master

Skill Levels	Managerial Needs
Novice: Thumbnail • performance slow & jerky • attention to rules/facts • works with the book in hand • heavy learner *Managerial Problem:* the employee gets little reinforcement from the task	**Novice:** Training • understanding requirements & routines • reviewing requirements & routines • narrow policy/practice gap • often handled in groups • new employees or new requirements
Beginner: Thumbnail • performance faster & smoother • begins rule fade (acting automatically) • patterns not mentioned in rules • uses book less frequently • learner *Managerial Problem:* the employee experiences embarrassments	**Beginner:** Coaching • understands the requirements need to be accomplished by the employee • provides tips & suggestions • information is the key
Journey person: Thumbnail • performance usual in terms of speed & smoothness • rule fade mostly complete • selecting most important cues • calculated, educated risk taking • uses book only for exceptions • learner/teacher *Managerial Problem:* the employee may think it's the end	**Journeyperson:** Teaching • mastering requirements & routines • improving requirements & routines • pass along information • set standards • advising, stating, deflecting & reorganizing • provide suggestions • the employee studies on her or his own • checks in with the teacher for review
Expert: Thumbnail • performance becomes fluid • rule fade complete • calculation & rationality diminish • no plan is permanent • attention shifts with cues • holistic, intuitive grasp • can write the book • teacher *Managerial Problem:* the employee becomes locked in their own expertise; possible "culture lock"	**Expert:** Educating • questions/improves routines & requirements, as possible • brings best practices from elsewhere
Master: Thumbnail • performance is seamless • exactly the right speed; appears effortless • understands the deep structure of the effort • holistic recognition of cues • performance is solid, confident & sure • deeply understand • trust self & the process; let process flow; enter as needed • beyond the book *Managerial Problem:* finding, arranging, & managing access to the Master's knowledge & self	**Master:** Mentoring • employee growth is the focus • looking to the future • personal connection with employee • begins when one goes beyond her/his job responsibilities in a voluntary, caring, sharing & helping relationship • one prepares to work with mentees across the whole mentoring spectrum from participating in employer sponsored formal programs to creating interpersonal informal relationships • one mentors all associates according to their special needs.

Figure 35

Conclusion

Most of us are novices at some things and masters of others. It is key for managerial supervisors to accomplish two tasks. First, ask where you are with respect to the activities at hand. We all think of ourselves as masters, but honesty suggests that perhaps we should take a closer look. We do not have to be "over" someone in the flow channel to guide them. That is because the managerial job is essentially one of direction and coordination rather than performance. Orchestra conductors routinely conduct many musicians who are better at playing their particular instrument than the conductor is at playing the same instrument. It is good to keep that in mind.

The second task is to have a two pronged approach to supervision and management. One prong, as it were, is to use those with whom you work (subordinates, peers, superiors, and externals) appropriately. That is the "at a point in time" approach. Over time, though, you can be aware that they are likely (as are you) to drift off into the area of boredom as their skills increase faster than their challenges. You need to help them undertake new challenges. That is the other prong. (And, of course, you need to be aware of those times when challenges rise so fast that skill lags and anxiety occurs.) In each case with a skill lag or challenge lag, management is needed.

Part 7 - Chapter 16

FLAMEOUT, CALAMITY, AND SUPERCALAMITY

Introduction

Managers lose their way and their jobs all the time. When "you lose your way" as a manager, you engage in behaviors that cause you to lose your job, be passed over for promotion, or sent to wherever your organizational Siberia is. The precipitating behaviors that immediately cause these things to happen to you is terminal derailment. I call the predisposing activities leading to derailment as periderailment.

Derailment

There has been a good bit of attention to the issue of derailment and the reasons for it. Van Velsor and Leslie (1995) have done the most extensive work on this issue, though their work seems to combine both periderailment and derailment. Their work focuses on executives, with an emphasis on the top person. However, everything they say applies to managers as an entire group, not just the most senior manager (although they are, in many ways, more at risk because they have less supervision). They have explored a range of causes of derailment and I have organized them into two groups as follows:

> 1. precipitating/catalytic
>
> 2. predisposing/antecedent.

1.) Precipitating / Catalytic

Precipitating/Catalytic causes are as follows:

Ethical Breeches

Ethical breeches involve managers who steal from the organization, or commit other crimes for which they are arrested and after which they are usually let go.

Betrayal of Trust

Managers who use the special knowledge they have as managers (either through personal exchange or access to records) for personal advancement are usually let go. Lying about one's credentials also fits here.

Specific Behavioral Problems

Sometimes behavioral problems get in the way of work. Sexual harassment and acting out is one area. Sexual harassment is illegal, and sexual acting out, which is often very close, creates problems even if it does not fit into the "hostile workplace" area of sexual harassment. Substance abuse, (drugs and alcohol) is also deeply problematic.
Failure to adapt to a new boss's approach and style is also very problematic. Sometimes the new boss is just too different. These adjustmental difficulties can often be compounded if you were a candidate for that job but did not get it.

2. Predisposing / Antecedent

Causes of derailment are usually pretty specific and well known in the organization. Most of the time members of the organization wonder, "What took so long?" Predisposing causes (behavioral styles that lead to derailment) are a bit more subtle, nuanced, and complex. They include organizational, interpersonal and intrapersonal elements. Organizational elements include: failure to build a team and delegate, failure to think strategically, over reliance on a narrow circle of advisors, and failure to know the business and deliver positive results. Interpersonal elements include an abrasive style, which is problematic in itself and drives away employees and stops information sharing. Intrapersonal elements include a low emotional intelligence quotient and thus a failure to manage one's own emotions. Based on my observations and research, several dispositions emerge (listed 1 - 5) which can set the manager on the slippery slope of periderailment. Once on that slope, it is very difficult to avoid derailment itself. (Tropman and Shaefer, 2004)

1) From We to Me

Working in organizations requires working through others, and with others. The higher you go, the more you may experience a diminishment of the "we" and the enhancement of the "me." These are called attribution problems; self -attribution becomes more important than ever. You may feel that you are making all the key decisions and everyone else is just a peon.

2) From Observing Ego to Feedback Deafness

People at the top often come to have inflated and skewed ideas about their own prowess and importance. The observing ego is that part of our ego that monitors our personal behavior and makes appropriate adjustments to keep ourselves on a more or less steady path. Think of driving as an example. As we drive, we are constantly alert for other drivers, pedestrians, animals, weather, etc and adjusting our driving behavior. Someone who does not do these things, who bulldozes ahead regardless, is a great danger on the road, and also in an organization. An example of this is when a virtuoso performance becomes a solo performance. Experts and masters are especially prone to this problem.

3) From Substance to Substance Abuse

In many cases these managers become substance abusers. Excessive use of substances (alcohol and drugs) sometimes has dramatic negative results even though it is something that develops over time. Hence, it can be both predisposing and precipitating.

4) From Need to Greed

Employees, managers, and executives in the nonprofit sector usually are compensated at a lower scale than their training and the importance of their jobs to society merit. It is a sector wide problem that is of great importance to the society as a whole. On an individual basis, however, one can, over time, feel put upon and used, and then, perhaps, abused. This feeling set may lead one to take a skewed view toward ones's agency. An early "rectification" often involves giving oneself a raise by working less. This approach can escalate to other small things, like appropriating agency supplies and equipment for personal use. But it may expand to misuses of discretionary accounts and expense account padding to credit card misuse and co-mingling of agency funds. I think of these behaviors as greed.

5) From At the Top to Over the Top

Another problem managers face as they experience promotion is that they experience less and less control over themselves. Managers increasingly become, effectively, the only controller of their own behavior. Hence the opportunity for the abuses listed in "need to greed" can develop.

Conclusion

When supervisory managers, project managers and middle managers move up the ladder of the organization (which is one kind of success, as I will discuss in the next chapter) there is an increase in responsibility. Along with that is an increase in potential problems.

The rocks in the agency stream become harder to see and more jagged. Opportunities for specific behaviors that have career ending implications increase. Even more difficult to spot are those developing behavioral styles that are both problematic in themselves and can lead to specific acts that cause problems.

Part 7 - Chapter **17**

SECURING MANAGERIAL SUCCESS

Introduction

All managers – all of us – desire success. It is "the American dream." Success is a premiere driver, if not the driver, of the American Psyche. It was what eluded Willy Lowman in "Death of A Salesmen." None of us want to be the "low man" on the totem pole or bottom rung on the social ladder. We like our success big – the bigger the better. In the land of Big MACs, 7 figure bonuses, a 14,000 square foot hideaway (for two), and Humvees, it is almost as if size really does matter. The focus on **big** and **more** begs the question of balance and proportion. My classes have interviewed "successful" executives for dozens of years. Many of these respondents regret their overemphasis on work. They lament their missed anniversaries, kid's birthdays, games, plays, and the like. The old Cat Stevens song, "The Cat's in the Cradle" speaks to the Dad with no time, but promising something later: "We'll have a good time then, son, we'll have a good time then." Now in later midlife, these icons feel hollow, and sense that "real" success might have eluded them. Others feel that success is always ahead of them – whatever they achieve is tainted by their very possession of it. It is like the old line from Groucho Marx, "I would never want to belong to a club that would have me in it." Among the many problems with "success" is the question, What IS it, anyway? This chapter suggests there are two ways to think about success, as well as, a tool to monitor your progress toward "it" and your drift away from "it."

Success as Balance and Proportion of Goals

If you look on Amazon.com you find over 17,000 listings for books on "success". (Google has 590 million!)There are thousands of quotes about success. Much of the thinking on success emphasizes the point I mentioned before – big, public recognition of some achievement or series of achievements. Certainly, if you have more than anyone of a desired good, you are a "success" in conventional terms. Many say that having more, "trumps" failures. (And isn't it interesting that "The Donald" is named Trump?)

But there is also the sense that too much of a good thing is, well, a bad thing. "Money is the root of all evil" (Bible: New Testament St. Paul, in 1 Timothy, 6:10....) is one popular example of "too much of muchness." Power, as well, is a problem in large amounts. "Power corrupts; absolute power corrupts absolutely," is a famous phrase from Lord Acton. We are also aware of people destroyed by status seeking, by desperate attempts to get the top job, etc. It seems that success might be better seen as a balance among elements, rather than a huge amount of one element.

Based upon my interviews with lots of executives, I have provisionally concluded that there are five goal sectors, which need to be balanced for a person to "feel" success.

1) **Personal goals** that one has, such as personal development, securing a degree, continuing education, and so on. Also important are the maintaining of personal relationships, other than family and committed partners. Attention to this is what is called "sharpening your saw."

2) **Partners and family members**. They need attention and help and our assistance in achieving their own success.

3) **Work**. Part of work is of course the job, those things we do between 8 and 5 (or whenever and whenever, depending upon your schedule). But in many areas, and the human services is certainly one of them, there is always that "extra" that you do, and that needs to be done. This area is especially difficult in human services because, as I discussed in Chapter 3, the pressure of human need and human problems is always upon us.

4) **Civic activities**. Civic activities involve helping out in our neighborhood, community, state, and nation. Each of us has a citizen role and democracy cannot function if each of us does not pay some attention to improving the common weal. There are of course "social loafers" among us, those who always let others do the community work. But we do not want to be among that group. (Some activities here might be agency citizenship – cleaning the refrigerator in the staff lounge; helping with holiday decorations, etc.)

5) Finally, the **X factor**, which is personal as well, but relating to our unique interests and passion (being a good knitter, writing poetry, etc..) These are goals that one may share with others, but they are important. We might think of these as "hobbies" perhaps, or areas of avocation that are of great importance.

There is no specific set of proportions for these five goals that are right for everyone. Each of us needs to work out an appropriate balance, and rework that balance as our life changes. The one imperative is that you should not let any one goal area slip below about 10 % (Figure 36). This is most especially true in personal and X factors – they usually go first if pressures mount; family goes next. Apart from some minimum distribution, what is important is that you imagine an ideal distribution and then check it against what is "really going on."

The Index of Difference as a Success Balance Assay

Life Area	Ideal [1]	Real [2]	Absolute Difference [3]
Personal & Relationship	20%	0%	20%
Partner/Family	30%	10%	20%
Work	30%	90%	60%
Civic	15%	0%	15%
The X Factor	5%	0%	5%
Total	100%	100%	120%/2=60%

Figure 36

For illustrative purposes, I am using the same application we went through before in terms of schedule control and strategic focusing. Although we went through the calculation previously, let me review it again. First, you fill out the ideal column with percentages that total to 100%. That is all the time you have. Then you look at your actual expenditure of time and fill that in the "real" column. The figures represented above are typical for busy executives and managers. In Column 3 you record the absolute difference between Columns 1 and 2 (disregarding sign).

Finally, you sum up Column 3 and divide by two (to take care of the sign issue). The resulting number (in Figure 36 is 60%), is the Index of Difference. It shows how "out of whack" your ideal/real relationship is. Generally numbers below 10% are good; the higher the number, the more difference there is, the more reallocation is needed and the more stress will exist unless that reallocation is accomplished.

The 60% does not say where the manager should make the reallocation, of course. Perhaps the ideal allocation is unrealistic and you need to make adjustments there. More than likely, this is a scenario in which you drift into a skewed distribution in the real column without really thinking about it. Hence, achieving more control over your actual allocation of time/effort is the way to go.

What makes for success, then, at least in my argument here, is a balance comfortable to you and those around you (in terms of emphases). As with time, success factors tend to drift away. Balance is something that needs work but it will be well worth the effort.

Conclusion

Success is something all managers crave, and I believe is in the grasp of many, if thought about correctly. Dying with the most toys is not, for most, a measure of success. However, if that floats your particular boat, knock yourself out! Most of the work I have done suggests that a managed balance leads to long term success in life, very much as it does in your financial portfolio.

As you move through your career, there will be changes in your balance. The "ideal" column will become reweighted. Pressures will cause you to discover "Allocations" in the "Real" column that you did not plan. You will need constant oversite and adjustments. But that's management!

Managing is, as Peter Vail said, a performing art (Vail, 1989). It is fun to bring people and resources together and produce outcomes, events, innovations, and results. Desirable conclusions (because results and outcomes can be bad, like decisions) do rarely happen by themselves. Guidance is essential for systems and/or agencies to function well and to continually improve that functioning. Management provides that guidance even though managers are unappreciated. Bad managers are usually noticed because employees flee them, results are poor, and they are continually off-loading responsibilities on "the system" or whatever. Good managers are the unsung heroes of the organizational enterprise.

As you can see, there is a lot to know to be a good manager and the material here is just a start, but it is a good start. By the time you have mastered even some of this material you will be so far ahead of your contemporaries that you will be promoted to a post of Executive Leadership. That is another Challenge!

APPENDIX 1

A Table of Topics: A review of popular books in that focus on supervisory management and their connection to this book

Chapters in Tropman	Supervision: A Decision Making Approach (Gambrill & Stein, 1983)	Competent Supervision (Middleman & Rhodes, 1985)	The 21st Century Supervisor (Humphrey & Stokes, 2000)	Supervisor's Portable Answer Book (Fuller, 1990)	What Every Supervisor Should Know 6th Edition (Bittel & Newstrom, 1992)	The First Time Supervisor's Survival Guide (Fuller, 1995)	The New Supervisor 5th Edition (Broadwell & Dietrich, 1998)	Managing Human Resources in the Human Services: Supervisory Challenges (Perlmutter, et al, 2001)
Chapter 1				X	X	X		
Chapter 2	X							
Chapter 3	X			X			X	X
Chapter 4				X				
Chapter 5	X		X	X	X	X	X	X
Chapter 6				X				
Chapter 7	X			X			X	
Chapter 8	X			X			X	
Chapter 9	X				X		X	X
Chapter 10		X	X	X	X	X		
Chapter 11							X	
Chapter 12	X				X		X	
Chapter 13			X				X	
Chapter 14			X	X			X	X
Chapter 15	X			X	X	X	X	X
Chapter 16						X		X
Chapter 17				X	X			

Resources for Appendix 1: The Tables of Contents of Popular Books on Supervisory Management

Gambrill, E. & Stein, T. (1983). Supervision: a decision making approach. Thousand Oaks, CA: Sage.

Intake and Initial Case Planning
Evaluating the Quality of Decision Making Within Outcomes Categories
Evaluating the Quality of Assessment
Evaluating the Quality of Decisions Made During Intervention
Coordinating Services
Encouraging Effective Staff Behavior
Arranging Training Programs
Interpersonal Decision Making Skills (Developing and Maintaining, and Improving)

Middleman, R. & Rhodes, G. (1985). Competent supervision. Englewood Cliffs: Prentice Hall.

Integrating
Humanizing
Managing Tension
Catalyzing

Service Delivery
Teaching
Career Socializing
Evaluating

Linkage
Administering
Advocating
Changing

Humphrey, B & J. Stokes (2000). The 21st century supervisor. San Francisco, CA: Jossey Bass.

People Skills
Communication
Team
Coaching

Technical Skills
Business Analysis
Continuous Improvement
Computer

Administrative Skills
Project management
Writing
Resource Management

Fuller, G. (1990). Supervisor's portable answer book. Englewood Cliffs: Prentice Hall.

Commonsense Communication
Difficult People
Employee Complaints
Discipline
Motivating Performance ((Pay, Promotions, Praise)
Overcoming Obstacles to Productivity
Hire/Fire
Working Outside Your Dept
Bearing Up Under (managing) Your Boss

Bittel, L. & J. Newstrom (1992). What every supervisor should know. 6th ed.
New York, NY: McGraw Hill.

Planning and Control
Organizing, staffing and training
Activating the Work Force
Managing Problem performance
Improving Departmental productivity
Legal Concerns

Fuller, G. (1995). The first time supervisor's survival guide. Englewood Cliffs: Prentice
Hall.

Dealing with Employee Concerns
Managing Worker Job Performance
Distasteful Duties (Discipline, Layoff, Sexual Harassment,, Substance Abuse, Theft,
Difficult People)
Working with People Outside Your Department

Broadwell, M. & Dietrich, C.B. (1998). The new supervisor. 5th edition. Cambridge: Perseus Books.

Attitude(Toward Job, Boss, Subordinate)
Monitoring and Managing stress
Good Communications
Setting Up Work (Planning and Organizing)
Getting Work Done (Directing and Controlling)
Delegation
Problem Solving
Effective Meetings
Written and Oral Presentations
Team Building

Perlmutter, F., Baily, D. & Netting, F.E. (2001). Managing human resources in the human services: supervisory challenges. New York, NY: Oxford.

Responding to Legal Mandates
Building Strategic Alliances
Humanizing Technology
Facilitating Communication
Supporting Diversity
Creating and Sustaining Teams
Motivating, Appraising, Rewarding
Protecting Managers as Workers
Evaluating Program Effectiveness

APPENDIX 2

ELECTRONIC RESOURCES

www.amanet.org/selfstudy/super.htm

American Management Associations website which provides information on and links to training opportunities, events, seminars, and other resources

http://www.calib.com/nccanch/pubs/usermanuals/supercps/supercps.pdf

Specific article written by Thomas D. Morton and Marsha K. Salus about supervising child protective services caseworkers

http://www.allianceonline.org/

The Alliance for Nonprofit Management is the professional association of individuals and organizations devoted to improving the management and governance capacity of nonprofits - to assist nonprofits in fulfilling their mission.

The Alliance is a learning community that promotes quality in nonprofit capacity building. The Alliance convenes a major annual conference, networks colleagues year-round online, and provides member discounts on books and other publications. The Alliance provides visibility to its members in the online "Find a Consultant or Service Provider" directory, the People of Color Roster, and the print membership directory.

http://www.mapnp.org/library/

Free Management Library(SM) is a complete, highly integrated library for nonprofits and for-profits

http://www.cnmsocal.org/

The Center for Nonprofit Management is proud to celebrate 25 years of service to the nonprofit community. Since 1979, the Center has fostered healthy neighborhoods and communities by improving the performance of nonprofit organizations addressing critical issues and serving underserved populations.

Current Services

Nonprofit Directions Job Listing: Job listing newsletter for Southern California nonprofits.

Professional Development Seminars: Classes focusing specifically on the needs of the nonprofit sector.

Consulting: Services ranging from strategic planning to board development.

Publications: Books that address the most critical needs of the nonprofit sector.

NPower Los Angeles: Helping nonprofits use technology to expand the reach and impact of their work.

Compensation & Benefits Survey: Annual survey of nonprofit job salaries and benefits.

Nonprofit Resource Library: Identify and research potential funding sources.

Prism e-newsletter: Sign up for their free, monthly newsletter.

http://www.angonline.org/index.asp

The Alliance for Nonprofit Governance (ANG) works to raise the standards of governance of nonprofit organizations, particularly in New York. Its varied members include individuals and organizations ranging from nonprofit umbrella agencies and consultants to funders, regulators, academics, lawyers and accountants. They are all committed to working collaboratively:

- To discuss and reach consensus on what effective nonprofit governance means;
- To raise awareness about the importance of effective governance and provide access to helpful resources;
- To develop evidence that effective governance enhances organizational effectiveness; and
- To further develop the ANG as a collaborative partnership able to achieve its goals and objectives.

http://news.gilbert.org/

Nonprofit Online News and News of the Online Nonprofit Community

www.amacombooks.org/books/catalog/MGS.htm

List of books on supervisions and management

GLOSSARY OF TERMS

Beginner – performs tasks faster and smoother than a novice worker, does not use the book as often, and begins "rule fade".

Career coaching - the process though which you develop a career path.

Career pathing - the process through which individuals, alone or with a human resources professional, chart their career development over a series of jobs.

Critical Path - a period between two tasks such that, the amount of time you have to do it is exactly the amount of time you need to do it.

Derailment – the precipitating behaviors that immediately cause a person to loose their job, be passed over for promotion, or sent to whatever their organizational Siberia is.

Expert – performance is fluid, quick, and sure. Decision-making tools such as structured decision-making become an integral part of their conceptual framework.

Gantt charting - adds start, duration, and finish times to all the tasks that comprise the processes phase (but can also apply to outputs and outcomes).

Index of Difference – the difference between your real and ideals that shows how "out of whack" your ideal/real relationship is.

Job coaching - deals with items and concerns with respect to the specific job you have at any one time.

Journeyperson - performance is notable for its speed and smoothness, selects only the most important cues, and ignores "noise."

KnOWER (Knowledge, Organization, Write, Evaluate, and Rewrite) - provides a useful way to think through the issues and touch all the proper bases when drafting written communication.

Logic modeling - represents a horizontal flow of project subtasks from the initiating task to the concluding task.

Master - performance is seamless, solid, confident, and sure. Their work is done at exactly the right speed and it appears effortless. Masters understand the deep structure of effort.

Meeting Masters - individuals who run meetings right.

Middle Manager - has more than one project, or a much larger project, that you are responsible for. The work of middle management involves attention to the mission of the agency and is made up of bundles of project tasks, which are in turn comprised of jobs and assignments.

Novice - perform tasks in a slow and uneven manner, pay close attention to rules and facts, and does many things by the book.

Periderailment - the predisposing activities leading to derailment.

PERT (Program, Evaluation and Review Technique) - a way to identify and track project activities over time.

Project Manager - responsible for the completion of a project in the agency, which involves sequencing or linking jobs and tasks, and supervise one or more direct reports (or people assigned to work on that project).

Supervisory Manager - in charge of one or more persons for the purpose of assisting them with the accomplishment of their jobs and assuring that their assignments are completed in a timely fashion, and according to law and policy.

SOURCES

Abrams, M. (1990) "Mental Fitness Strategies" Compass (November) pp.72-74

Arygris, C. (1985) *Strategy, Change and Defensive Routines.* Upper Saddle River, NJ. Longman

Baken, J. (2004) *The Corporation: the Pathological Pursuit of Profit and Power.* New York-Free Press

Benedict, R. (1934) *Patterns of Culture Boston.* Houghton Mifflin

Bianchi, Allison,(2004) "A Review of "Emotions and Sociology" Jack Barbalet, ed.Oxford UK,   Malden, MA Blackwell. *In Contemporary Sociology* 33, 3 (May)pp.313-314

Bittel, L. & Newstrom, J. (1992) *What Every Supervisor Should Know 6th* New York: McGraw Hill

Blanchard, K., Eddington, D.W., & Blanchard, M. (1989). *One minute manager gets fit.* Quill.

Bramson, R. (1981) *Coping with Difficult People*   New York: Doubleday

Bramson, R. (1992) *Coping with Difficult Bosses* New York. Fireside/Simon Shuster

Broadwell,M. & Dietrich, C. (1998) *The new superisor* 5th ed. Cambridge: Perseus Books

Buckingham, M. & Coffman, C. (1999). *First Break All the Rules.* New York, NY: Simon & Schuster.

Cary, Benedict, "Fear in the Workplace: The Bullying Boss" New York Times, Science Times Section, June 22, 2004. pd1ff

Cohen, M. D., March, J. G. & Olson J. P. Olsen. *A garbage can model of organizational choice.* Administrative Science Quarterly, 17:1--25, 1972.

Covey, W., (1990) *The Seven Habits Of Highly Effective People.* New York: Fireside,

Davis, S. (1987, 1996). *Future perfect.* Reading, PA: Addison-Wesley.

Deming, W.E. (1982) <u>Out of crisis Cambridge</u>, MIT Press

Douglas, E. (1998). STRAIGHT TALK: *Turning Communication Upside Down for Strategic Results at Work*. Palo Alto, CA Davis Black

De Vries, M. K and D. Miller (1984;1990) *The Neurotic Organization: Diagnosing and Changing Counter Productive Styles of Management*. San Francisco: Jossey Bass

Frumkin, P. (2002) *On Being Nonprofi* Cambridge, MA. Harvard University Press.

Fuller, G. (1990) *Supervisor's Portable Answer Book* Englewood Cliffs, Prentice Hall, 1990

Fuller, G. (1995) *The First Time Supervisors Survival Guide* Englewood Cliffs, Prentice Hall,

Gambrill, E. & Stein, T. (1983) *Supervision: A Decision Making Approach* . Thousand Oaks CA: Sage,

Grey, J. (1992) *Men are from Mars; Women are from Venus* New York, Harper Collins.

Goleman,D. (1995) *Emotional Intelligence* New York, Dutton

Hein, Sheila, (2004) "Silence Your Inner Critic" Real Simple (August) pp. 188-190.

Harvey, J. (1988). *The Abilene Paradox and Other Meditations on Management. San Francisco, CA: Jossey-Bass. The original publication of the Abilene Paradox appeared as: "The Abilene Paradox: The Management of Agreement," in Organizational Dynamics (Summer 1974) pp. 63-80*

Henlein, R. (1961) *Strangers in a Strange Land* New York. Avon

Hochschild, A.R, (1983;2003) The Managed Heart. Berkley. University of California

Hochshild, A.R. (1989;2003) the Second Shift. New York Renquin

Humphrey, B & Stokes, J. (2000) *The 21st Century Supervisor*. San Francisco, CA: Jossey Bass.

Janis, I. (1983) *Groupthink: Psychological Studies of Policy Decisions and Fiascoes* Boston: Houghton Mifflin.

Janis, I. & Mann, L. (1977) *Decision Making* New York: The Free Press.

Johnson, D.(2000) *Creating Names in the NonProfit Sea*. New York Times.

Kane, J. (1970, August). Dynamics of the Peter principle. pp. B800-B812.

Kerr, S. (1995). On the folly of rewarding A while hoping for B. Academy of Management Executive, 9(1), 7-14.

Kanter, R. (1977). *Men and women of the corporation.* New York: Basic Books.

Keegan, R. and L. Lahey (2001). How We Talk Can Change The Way We Work. San Francisco. Jossey Bass.

Kiersey, D. & Bates, M. (1984) *Please Understand Me* Del Mar, CA: Prometheus Nemesis Books,

Kidder, T. (1981) *The Soul of a New Machine* Boston: Little Brown

March, J.G. & Simon, H. (1959) *Organizations* New York: Wiley

Middleman R., and G. Rhodes, (1985) *Competent Supervision.* Englewood Cliffs: Prentice Hall,

McNamara, C. http://www.managementhelp.org/np_progs/np_mod/org_frm.htm

Mintzberg, H. (1989) *Mintzberg on Management* New York. Free Press/Macmmillan

Myers, G. *When It Hits the Fan* (1981) New York: Mentor Books.

Nelson, B. (1994). *1001 Ways to Reward Employees.* New York, NY: Workman Publishing.

Parsons, T. (1960) *Structure and Process in Modern Societies* Glencoe, IL. The Free Press.

Perlmutter, F., Baily D. & Netting F.(2001). *Managing Human Resources In The Human Services: Supervisory Challenges* New York, Oxford

Peter, L. (1970). The Peter Principle. New York: Bantam.

Peter, L. (1972). The Peter Prescription. New York: Bantam.

Peters, T., & Waterman, R. (1982). *In search of excellence.* New York: Harper & Row.

Pollan, S. (1996) *Lifescripts : What to Say to Get What You Want in 101 of Life's Toughest Situations* New York : Macmillan USA, 1996.

Portny, S. (2000). *Project Management for Dummies.* Wiley CDA

Quinn, Robert (1988) *Beyond Rational Management.* San Francisco: Jossey Bass

Rittel, H. & Weber, M. (1973) ""Dilemmas in a General Theory of Planning" Policy Sciences (July), 4 (2) : 155-169

Sayles, L. & Chandler, M., *Managing Large Systems* (1971) New York, Harper Collins. (Reprinted in 1992 by Transaction Books.)

Scott, A.O.,(2004) "Giving Corporations the Psychoanalytic Treatment" the *New York Times* Wednesday, June 30. p.B5

Schmitz, C. & Parson, B. http://www.insites.org/documents/logmod.htm

Solomon, M., (1980) *Working with Difficult People* Paramus, NJ. Prentice Hall.

Speer, Jack."Doing America's Dirty Work." Morning Edition . National Public Radio, . 29 August 2002. Transcript. 17 Jan 2005 <www.npr.org>.

Stone, D., Patton B. & Heen S., (1999) *Difficult Conversations*. New York, Viking,

Tannen, Deborah, (1990) *You Just Don't Understand: Men And Women In Conversation* New York: Harper Business, 1990

Thurber, J. (1945). The Thurber Carnival. New York. Harper

Tichy, N. M., & Devanna, M. A. (1986). *The transformational leader.* New York: Wiley.

Tropman, J. (2002) *The Catholic Ethic and the Spirit of Community*   Georgetown University Press,

Tropman, J. (1986) *Conflict in Culture: Permissions versus Controls and Alcohol Use in American Society*. Lanham, MD: University Press of America,

Tropman, J. (1995) *The Catholic Ethic in American Society*. San Francisco, CA: Jossey-Bass

Tropman, J. (1984) Policy Management in the Human Services. New York. Columbia

Tropman, J., (1989) *American Values and Social Welfare*. Englewood Cliffs: Prentice-Hall.

Tropman, J., (2002) *Making Meetings Work* 2nd ed. Thousand Oaks, CA: Sage

Tropman, John (1984) *Policy Management in the Human Services* . New York. Columbia University Press

Tropman, J and Shaefer, Luke (2004). Flameout at the top: Executive C in the Nonprofit Sector. <u>Administration in Social Work</u>: 28, 34

Tuchman, B. Tuchman (1984). *The March of Folly: From Troy to Vietnam.* New York: Knopf.

Vail, P. (1989). *Managing as a Performing Art: New Ideas for a World of Change.* San Francisco, CA: Jossey-Bass.

Van Velsor & Leslie, (1995) "Why Executives Derail: Perspectives Across Time and Cultures" *The Academy of Management Executive.* 9, 4 (November) pp. 62-73

Vidich, A. & Bensman, J. (2000[1958]) *Small Town in Mass Society* Champaign, IL: The University of Illinois Press

Weber, Max (1946) *From Max Weber* tr. By H. Gearth and C.W.Mills. New York, Oxford.

Weick, K. (1995)*Sensemaking in Organizations* Thousand Oaks, CA. Sage Publications.

Whetten, D. & Cameron, K. (2005). *Developing Management Skills*, 6th ed. Prentice Hall: Upper Saddle River, NJ,

RESOURCES - BOOKS

Adams, S. (1996) <u>Dogbert's top secret management handbook</u>. New York: Harper

Adams, S. (1996) <u>The Dilbert principle</u> New York: Harper

Argyris, C. (1964). <u>Integrating the individual and the organization</u>. New York: John Wiley & Sons.

Argyris, C. (1969). Individual actualization in complex organizations. In F. D. Carver & T. Sergiovanni (Eds.). <u>Organizations and human behavior: Focus on schools</u>. New York: McGraw-Hill Book Co..

Argyris, C. (1982). <u>Reasoning, learning and actions: Individual and organizational</u>. San Francisco: Jossey-Bass.

Autrey, J. (1991). <u>Love and Profit</u>. New York: Avon.

Baker, W. (1993). <u>Networking smart</u>. New York: McGraw Hill.

Bass, B. (1990). <u>Stodgill's handbook of leadership</u> (3rd ed.). New York: Free Press.

Behn, R. (1991). <u>Leadership Counts</u>. Cambridge: Howard University Press.

Behn, R. (1991). <u>Leadership Counts</u>. Cambridge: Howard University Press.

Bennis, W., & Nanus, B. (1985). <u>Leaders</u>. New York: Harper.

Block, P. (1993) <u>Stewardship</u>. San Francisco: B?K

Bohlman, L., & Deal, T. (1991). <u>Reframing organizations</u>. San Francisco: Jossey-Bass.

Bowen, W., 1994) <u>Inside the Boardroom</u>. New York: Wiley

Collins, B., & Guetzkow, H. (1964). <u>A social psychology of group processes for decision making</u>. New York: John Wiley and Sons.

Csikszentmihalyi, M. (1990). <u>Flow: The psychology of optimal experience</u>. New York: Harper.

deBono, E. (1970). <u>Six thinking hats</u>. Reading, MA: Addison & Wesley.

DePree, M. (1993). <u>Leadership jazz</u>. New York: Doubleday.

Drucker, P. (1985). Innovation and entrepreneurship. New York: Harper and Row.

Drucker, P. (1993). Post capitalist society. New York: Harper Business.

DuBrin, A., (1996) Reengineeering Survival Guide. Cincinnati: Thompson Executive Press

Egan, G. (1994). Working the shadow side. San Francisco: Jossey Bass.

Flamholtz, E. G. (1985). How to make the transition from an entrepreneurship to a professionally managed firm.

Galbraith, J. (1982, Winter). Designing the innovating organization. Organizational Dynamics, 5-25.

Garfield, C. (1992) Second to none. Homewood: Irwin

Goldratt, E., & Cox, J. (1986). The goal: The process of ongoing improvement. Croton-on Hudson, NY: North River Press.

Goleman, D. (1995). Emotional Intelligence. New York: Bantam.

Gordon, W. J. J. (1973). Synectics: The development of creative capacity. New York: Collier.

Grove, A. (1983). (1983). High output management. New York: Random House.

Harrigan, B. (1992). Games your mother never taught you. New York: Warner.

Heifetz, R.,(1994) Leadership without easy answers. Cambridge: Harvard

Heller, R., The superchiefs (1992) New York: Dutton

Hesselbein, F. (Ed.), (1996). The Leader of the Future. San Francisco: Jossey-Bass.

Holcombe, M., & Stein, J. (1981). Writing for decision makers. Memos and reports with a competitive edge. Belmont: Wadsworth.

Houle, C. O. (1989) Governing boards. San Francisco: Jossey Bass.

Janis, I., & Mann, L. (1977). Decision making. New York: The Free Press.

Johnson, W. (1979). Muddling toward frugality. Boulder: Shambhale.

Josefowitz, N. (1980). Paths to Power. Redding, MA: Addison Wesley.

Kanter, R. (1982). The change masters. New York: Simon & Schuster.

Katz, D., & Kahn, R. (1978). The social psychology of organizations (2nd ed.). New York: Wiley.

Levering, R. (1990). A great place to work. New York: Avon.

Levinson, H. (1981). The executive. Cambridge, MA: Harvard University Press.

Levinson, H. (1983, June). Getting along with the boss. Across the Board.

Lynn, L. E. (1981). Managing the public's business: The job of the government executive. New York: Basic Books.

Mackenzi, A. (1990). The time trap. New York: AMACOM.

Malburg, C. (1991). How to fire your boss. New York: Burley Books.

March, J. G. (Ed.). (1965). The handbook of organizations. Chicago: Rand McNally.

Maurer, J., et. al. (1995) The Encyclopedia of Business Detroit, Gale

McGregor, D. (1960). The human side of enterprise. New York: McGraw Hill.

Miller, D. (1990). The Icarus Paradox: How Exceptional Companies Bring About Their Own Downfall. New York: Harper-Collins.

Miller, L. (1984). American spirit: Visions of a new corporate culture. New York: Morrow, 1984).

Mills, D. (1985, July/August). Planning with people in mind. Harvard Business Review, 97-105.

Mintzberg, H. (1976, July/August). Planning on the left side and management on the right. Harvard Business Review.

Mintzberg, H. (1994). The Rise and Fall of Strategic Planning. New York: The Free Press.

Morita, A. (1987). Made in Japan. New York: Dutton.

Morrison, A. (1992) The new leaders: guidelines on leadership diversity in America. San Francisco: Jossey Bass

Myers, R., Ufford, P., & Magill, M. S. (1988). On site analysis: A practical approach to organization change. Etobicoke, Ontario: OSCA (416-626-0600).

Naisbitt, J.and P. Auberdene (1990). Megatrends2000. New York: Warner.

Ouchi, W. (1982). Theory Z. New York: Avon.

Parkinson, C. N. (1957). Parkinson's law and other studies in administration. New York: Houghton Mifflin.

Parsons, T. (1963). Suggestions for a sociological approach to the theory of organizations. In A. Etzioni (Ed.). Complex organizations: A sociological reader. New York: Holt, Rinehart and Winston.

Pascale, R. T., & Athos, A. (1981). The art of Japanese management. New York: Warner.

Pinchot, G. (1983). Intrapreneuring. New York: Harper & Row.

Powell, W. (1989). The non-profit sector. New Haven: Yale.

Primozic, K., Promozic, E., & Leben, J. (1991). Strategic choices: Success, survival or Sayonara! New York: McGraw Hill.

Quinn, R. (1988). Beyond rational management. San Francisco: Jossey-Bass.

Reed, S. (1993). The toxic executive. New York: Harper Business.

Reich, R. B. (1983). The next American frontier. New York: Times Books.

Rittel, Horst and Melvin Weber (1973) ""Dilemmas in a General Theory of Planning" Policy Sciences (July), 4 (2) : 155-169

Rothchild-Whitt, J. (1979). The collectivist organization: An alternative to rational bureaucratic model. American Sociological Review, 44, 509-527.

Rowan, R. (1986). The intuitive manager. Boston: Little and Brown.

Sales, L., & Chandler, M. (1971). The project manager: Organizational metronome. Managing larger systems. New York: Harper & Row.

Schneider, B. (Ed.), (1990). Organizational Culture and Climate. San Francisco: Jossey-Bass.

Schneider, B., editor (1990) Organizational climate and culture. San Francisco: Jossey Bass

Selznik, P. (1987). Leadership in administration. New York: Harper & Row.

Simon, H. V. Thompson and D. Smithburg. Public Adminisration (1991[1950])New Brunswick, NJ, Transaction

Spears, L. (Ed.), (1995). Reflections on Leadership. New York: Wiley.

Stechert, K. (1986). On your own terms: A woman's guide to working with men. New York: Vintage Books.

Synge, P. (1990). The fifth discipline. New York: Doubleday.

Vroom, V. H., & Yetton, P. W. (1973). Leadership and decision-making. Pittsburgh: University of Pittsburgh Press.

Wareham, J. (1991). The anatomy of a great executive. New York: Harper.

White, R., et. al., The Future of leadership: a whitewater revolution. London: Pittman

Van Velsor & Leslie, " "Why Executives Derail: Perspectives Across Time and Cultures" THE ACADEMY OF MANAGEMENT EXECUTIVE   (11/95)

Wissema, J. G., Van der Pol, H. V., & Messer, H. M. (1980, January, March). Strategic management archetypes. Strategic Management Journal, 37-47.

Zaleznik, A. (1990). The Managerial Mystique. New York: Harper.

Zander, A. (1982). Making groups effective. San Francisco: Jossey-Bass.

RESOURCES –ARTICLES

Barton, A. (1979). A diagnosis of bureaucratic maladies. American Behavioral Scientist, 22, 483-492.

Buhler Patricia M "A new role for managers: The move from directing to coaching" Supervision; Burlington; Oct 1998;; Volume: 59; Issue: 10; Start Page: 16-18

Cousins Roland B "Active listening is more than just hearing" Supervision; Burlington; Sep 2000;; Volume: 61; Issue: 9 Start Page: 14-15

Cole ,Michael "Become the leader followers want to follow" Supervision; Burlington; Dec 1999;; Volume: 60; Issue: 12; Start Page: 9-11

Fracaro, Ken "Two ears and one mouth" Supervision; Burlington; Feb 2001 Volume: 62; Issue: 2; Start Page: 3-5

Fracaro, Ken; "Empathy: A potent management tool" Supervision; Burlington; Mar 2001; Volume: 62; Issue: 3; Start Page: 10-13

Grassell, Milt; "How To Supervise Difficult Employees" Supervision; Burlington; Jul 1989; Volume: 50; Issue: 7; Start Page: 3

Lindo, David; "Will you ever get it right?" Supervision; Burlington; Dec 1999; Volume: 60; Issue: 12; Start Page: 6-8

Hull,William W "Passing the buck vs. making an assignment" Supervision; Burlington; Mar 1999;; Volume: 60; Issue: 3;Start Page: 6-7

O'Neil Michael A "How to implement relationship management strategies" Supervision; Burlington; Jul 2000;; Volume: 61; Issue: 7; Start Page: 3-4

Pollock ,Ted; "Sharpening your dialogue skills" Supervision; Burlington; Aug 2000; Volume: 61; Issue: 8; Start Page: 13-15

Pollan, Stephen M. Lifescripts : What to Say to Get What You Want in 101 of   Life's Toughest Situations New York : Macmillan USA, 1996.

Pulich, Marcia Ann "Revitalizing an Employee's Job Interest" Supervisory Management; Saranac Lake; Mar 1989; Volume: 34; Issue: 3; Start Page: 3

Ramsey, Robert D; "Do you have what it takes to be a mentor?" Supervision; Burlington;

Mar 1999; Volume: 60;Issue: 3;Start Page: 3-5

Shea, Gordon "Can a supervisor mentor?" <u>Supervision</u>; Burlington; Nov 1995;; Volume: 56;Issue: 11;Start Page: 3

Tropman, John (1989) "The Organizational Circle," *Administration in Social Work* 13, 1 (1989).

Tropman, J. and Schuester, K.R.,(2000) "The Concept of System Levels in Social Work" (with Kathrine Richards-Schuester) in P. Allen-Meares and Charles Garvin, eds, the *Handbook of Social Work Direct Practice* .Thousand Oaks: Sage

Weiss W H; "The art and skill of delegating" <u>Supervision</u>; Burlington; Sep 2000; Volume: 61; Issue: 9; Start Page: 3-5;

Woodruff, Michael J "Understanding & Supervising the Twentysomethings" <u>Supervision</u>; Burlington; Apr 1992;.; Volume: 53; Issue: 4; Start Page: 10

INDEX